THE ENNEAGRAM AND THE BIBLICAL COUNSELOR

By Rhenn Cherry

Association of Certified
Biblical Counselors

As we face the issues of sin and suffering in a broken world, we all need wisdom from God. Thankfully, the Lord has given us all that we need for life and godliness through His sufficient Word (2 Peter 1:3; 2 Timothy 3:16).

ACBC's Truth in Love resources are designed to bring the rich truth of God's character and promises to bear on the problems people face in everyday life. As you walk with others, seeking to minister the very words of God to them, we pray this booklet will be a resource that points you back to His truth and equips you to admonish the idle, encourage the fainthearted, and help the weak (1 Thessalonians 5:14).

Author
Rhenn Cherry is Director of Finances and Donor Relations at the Association of Certified Biblical Counselors and Adjunct Professor of Biblical Counseling at Midwestern Baptist Theological Seminary.

Personality tests have been around for quite a while, and many counselors have uncertainty about whether or not personality typing is appropriate for use in biblical counseling. The Enneagram is currently the most popular personality typing system among evangelical Christians. It has been promoted as an ancient tool that contains spiritual wisdom. But what are the theological roots of the Enneagram, and how do these foundations affect the decision to accept or reject the Enneagram? Should Christians embrace and employ the Enneagram as a ministry tool, or are there dangers associated with its use within the church and Christian institutions? An evaluation of the Enneagram's theology is helpful to address confusion about the suitability of using it in the context of an evangelical church.

First, we must acknowledge that every discipleship or counseling system incorporates an underlying philosophy. Every counseling system employs a way of thinking about life in order to better understand people with the hope of helping people. I am not claiming that those who utilize the Enneagram have faulty motives. In fact, that's often the first mistake that people make when critiquing a particular counseling approach or tool. Let us be clear that we are not criticizing people who use the Enneagram as if they have evil motives. That is not the case. In fact, I would say most people who counsel others have a heart desire to help people. They want to see people change. They want to find a system that they believe will help someone change. Sometimes, counselors turn to personality typologies and testing.

Some Christian organizations rely heavily on personality testing and typing for both hiring decisions and personal conflict management in a team environment. But the benefits associated with personality typologies are limited and do not tend to address the core issue of man's sinfulness and need of redemption. Secular philosophies and therapies have had much influence on churches and Christian institutions. It is wise for us to question whether or not these philosophies have an appropriate place in the evangelical community.

Personality tests and typing systems have notorious historical patterns of being fashionable or trendy for a limited amount of time only. In other words, they tend to have a limited shelf-life. Cutting-edge personality tests tend to be replaced by the next new system that comes along.

A Modern History of Some Personality Typing Systems

Man's desire to have some "objective" means to explain himself to himself is not new. Over the last 150-200 years in Western culture, there has been a lot of emphasis placed on developing new personality tests. These popular tests are really man's attempt to reduce his own complexity into a neat category. Personality tests typically produce results in the forms of labeling and grouping of individuals. And each test usually has its own unique vocabulary for describing who people are, according to that particular system.

Phrenology

If you and I lived 150 years or so ago, we would have been on the cutting edge of personality testing "science" if we had our heads read by a phrenologist. Phrenology was labeled the "science of the mind" during the mid-nineteenth century. The theory held that the shape and size of a person's cranium, or skull, was an indicator of their character or mental ability. According to the "science" of phrenology, when certain parts of the brain were well-used, they expanded and pushed up the skull and produced a noticeable bulge. And so, a trained expert phrenologist would feel a person's head bumps and rate them, quite subjectively, from one to seven in 37 different character or personality areas.

Phrenology, like other personality typing systems that would follow, developed its own vocabulary for describing these supposed personality traits. As early as the mid-1800s we see potential employers begin to require written phrenology reports from job candidates. The reports themselves were promoted as being impartial and reliable third-party evaluations. But they effectively took the place of personal recommendations. The famous poet and novelist Walt Whitman was a big proponent of phrenology, and even two United States presidents had their "heads read" by a phrenologist. So, you can see that while it became quite popular, phrenology required a trained expert to read the bumps on your head. A person could not evaluate their own personality.

Rorschach Ink Blots

Another personality test that became popular in America in the 1930s was the Rorschach ink blots that were formed by folding paper where ink drops had been placed. The Rorschach utilizes trained experts, usually psychologists or psychiatrists, to present ink blot cards and then record how the client describes what he sees. The Rorschach focuses not so much on what someone sees but more on how someone sees what they see. The ink blot tests gained popularity at notable universities like Columbia and Cornell, and they are still quite popular today in schools, prisons, and the military as a supposed means to delineate general personality characteristics. But again, the Rorschach, like phenology, requires a trained expert to interpret the results. A person could not evaluate their own personality.

Minnesota Multiphasic Personality Inventory (MMPI)

The Minnesota Multiphasic Personality Inventory (MMPI) was developed in the 1930s at a University of Minnesota mental hospital. Its current form today has well over 500 questions, and it was developed somewhat in response to the artistic nature of the Rorschach ink blots. The MMPI sought to provide a more "scientific" approach to defining one's personality traits, and its developers moved quite intentionally away from being considered a "test." The MMPI emphasized quantification in an effort to be considered scientific while avoiding being stereotyped as unscientific and artistic in nature, like the Rorschach. Even though it was originally designed to classify mental patients, the MMPI is still currently used to screen potential hires in an effort to predict who will be a good employee. But the MMPI is another example of a personality typing system that requires a trained expert. A person could not evaluate their own personality.

Myers-Briggs Type Indicator (MBTI)

Around the same time (1920s-1930s), a lady named Katharine Briggs was converted, literally, to Carl Jung's psychology and she set her efforts to bring Jung's theories to the masses. She developed a "tool" for people to categorize themselves into 1 of 16 personality types. Her daughter, Isabella Myers would eventually standardize this version of self-discovery with a questionnaire that became the current Myers-Briggs Type Indicator (MBTI). The Myers-Briggs further provided a way for people to use a self-reporting instrument or "indicator" to describe themselves. And this opened the door for them to talk and think about who they think they actually are, according to a set of questions that they answered about themselves. Although the Myers-Briggs indicator has lost much of its popularity, it still has a large number of faithful users.

A Shift from Expert Observation to Self-Evaluation

At this point, it would be logical to ask, who answers the questions on a Myers-Briggs questionnaire? Is it an expert who observes you? A psychiatrist or psychologist? A counselor? The answer, of course, is that the person being tested completes the questionnaire about themselves.

We should not lose sight of the significance of this point. We see in Myers-Briggs a shift in control *from* the trained experts of phrenology and the MMPI *to* the person who wants to know who he is. We begin to see the brilliance and genius, for lack of better words, of personality typologies like Myers-Briggs or the Enneagram. To some degree, these systems give people what they want: An understanding of themselves on their own terms. That is, to a large degree, people can be whoever they want to be (if you pay the fee). You are the one answering the questions about yourself. This is an important distinction of systems like the Enneagram. Whether you are taking an online test, reading a book about the Enneagram, or attending a workshop about the Enneagram, you are the arbiter of which label and group gets applied to you.

In summary, personality typing and testing makes swift judgments about people. And the trained experts or the tests themselves serve as an authority that assigns people a label and a group. And these labels and these groups are often welcomed by the people who take the tests. In other words, most people feel some type of false relief by being labeled and grouped. They sometimes enjoy a sense that a diagnosis has been made, and they are now included in a group with others with the same diagnosis.

But there is a danger in believing that because you have labeled a person, you therefore understand that person. Even more scary is the illusion that self-mastery comes from self-knowledge, according to a man-made system. We can all agree that the Enneagram is currently the most popular self-knowledge tool among Christians. But an evaluation of Enneagram theology face-to-face with orthodox evangelical theology really calls into question whether or not the Enneagram is appropriate for use in Christian churches and institutions.

The Enneagram

So, what exactly is the Enneagram? A proper explanation of the Enneagram must first distinguish between the symbol and the personality typology. The word itself is formed from the Greek words "ennea," which means nine, and "gramma," which means that which is drawn. There have been various 9-pointed symbols in existence throughout history, but the symbol that is currently identified as the 9-point Enneagram was brought to the Western world by a mystic named G.I. Gurdjieff in the early 1900s. It is worth noting that a mystic is someone who claims two main things: First, a mystic claims to have attained a level of divine insight or understanding that transcends ordinary human knowledge. And second, a mystic lays claim to communicate directly with the Divine, or God, and eventually become one *with* God. G.I. Gurdjieff was a mystic who supposedly learned of the Enneagram while in the Middle East. But Gurdjieff did not apply the Enneagram to personality. Instead, he taught the Enneagram in secret and maintained that it gave him and his students an understanding of *all* things. The Enneagram symbol was brought to the Western world by a mystic who applied no personality typology to the symbol.

A Not-So-Ancient Symbol Meets Modern Psychiatric Labels

The origin of the personality typology that is now so closely associated with the Enneagram

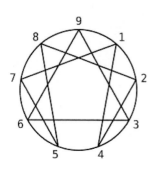

symbol can be traced back to two men, a Bolivian named Oscar Ichazo, and a Chilean named Claudio Naranjo. During the 1960s and 1970s, Naranjo was a psychiatrist who trained during under Fritz Perls, who is

recognized as the originator and developer of Gestalt therapy. This is significant, because a basic assumption of Gestalt therapy is that people can self-regulate themselves when they become self-aware and other-aware. According to Perls and his theory, this self-knowledge helps them understand what is happening in and around them. There is fundamental connection, according to Gestalt therapy, between self-mastery and self-knowledge.

Claudio Naranjo took nine personality types that he developed in conjunction with Oscar Ichazo and overlaid them onto the 9-pointed symbol.

Then he began teaching what he termed "Ennea-types" to Jesuit priests in the 1970s and eventually wrote *Ennea-type Structures: Self-Analysis for the Seeker* based on a transcription of his teachings on nine categories of neurosis.

Jesuit priests that Claudio Naranjo personally taught began using the Enneagram personality typology at their Catholic spiritual retreats in the late 1970s. Among Naranjo's students were priests Don Riso and Father Richard Rohr, who both began writing on the Enneagram. Riso developed online Enneagram type testing, and Rohr wrote *Discovering the Enneagram: An Ancient Tool for a New Spiritual Journey* in 1989. This demonstrates a progression of Catholic priests embracing the Enneagram and spiritualizing this secular personality typology. It is interesting that Richard Rohr would eventually re-title his original Enneagram book 20 years later as *The Enneagram: A Christian Perspective*. We now see how a clear path was cut that enabled a secular, non-Christian personality typology to be labeled as spiritual. In his retitled Enneagram work, Rohr even claimed that the Enneagram had Christian roots.

How the Enneagram Entered into Evangelical Churches

But why do the theological books of a Catholic priest matter to evangelicals? Do evangelical Christians really read the theology of Catholic priests like Richard Rohr? Richard Rohr, the Enneagram theologian, is important in all of this because he *personally* taught and mentored Enneagram authors Ian Cron and Suzanne Stabile who wrote *The Road Back to You*, and he also personally mentored Christopher Heuertz who wrote *The Scared Enneagram*. These authors dedicated their books to Richard Rohr, they quote him extensively throughout, and they consider him the theologian of the Enneagram system. These Enneagram books have been wildly popular among evangelical Christians, and Enneagram authors such as Beth and Jeff McCord have applied the system to marriage counseling in *Becoming Us: Using the Enneagram to Create a Thriving Gospel-Centered Marriage*. But is Enneagram theology truly consistent with an evangelical Christian view of God and man? And why does this matter?

It is important to pause here and define the term "evangelical." The secular world tends to broadly group religions that have some place for

Jesus as "Christian." But evangelical Christianity is distinct from other religions as it relates to the salvation of man. Evangelical Christianity maintains that the salvation of man involves repentance of a life of sin against a holy God and saving faith in the person and work of Christ alone. According to evangelicalism, supported by Scripture, there is no other means *available*, and no other means *required* for man to be reconciled to his Creator.

Richard Rohr, the Enneagram theologian, would not label himself as an evangelical Christian. But because Rohr has so strongly influenced Enneagram authors that are popular among evangelicals, the Enneagram, at least as evangelicals know it, is inextricably linked to the theology of the man Richard Rohr.

What should Christians think about it?

Discerning Christians should think about the Enneagram just like they do about *any* theory, practice, system, or teaching that they encounter. We must ask, what does this system say about God, about man, about sin, and about salvation? In other words, what is the problem, and what is the solution, according to this system or "tool"? How does the theology and anthropology of any teaching or system compare to the truth of the Bible? Christians must train themselves to ask these types of questions of everything. And so, if we are going to give fair analysis of this personality typology called the Enneagram, we must examine the theology of Richard Rohr and other Enneagram authors that he has influenced. This is important because Rohr has personally mentored and influenced the specific Enneagram authors who are most popular among evangelical Christians today.

Many Christians, pastors in particular, have not been able to take the time to investigate the underlying theology and anthropology of the Enneagram. And now many pastors find that there are people who are in their congregations who are using the Enneagram system, and those pastors honestly don't know what to do. They don't know what to make of this personality typology. The following evaluation of the Enneagram's doctrine of God and doctrine of man will prove helpful to those who have a limited amount of time to explore these important points. I was able to spend time investigating the theology of Richard Rohr as well as the Enneagram authors that he has influenced—namely Suzanne Stabile, Ian Cron, and Christopher Heuertz. My research revealed several points of theological and anthropological concern. I hope that you recognize that these two things—a doctrine of God and a doctrine of man—are always connected to each other.

Some may ask, "But if Richard Rohr is credited as being the Enneagram theologian, does he have specific views on God? Or are you just making some inferences about his theology?"

Yes, Richard Rohr is quite clear about his view on God. He unashamedly holds to a panentheistic theology. In fact, he goes out of his way to make sure that he is not confused with being a pantheist. Richard Rohr explicitly states in his 2019 New York Times bestseller, *The Universal Christ*, that he is a pan-*en*-theist. That is, he maintains and defends a theology that *God is in everything*. Rohr is careful to distinguish his panentheism from pantheism, which maintains that God *is* everything, or that everything *is* God. Rohr maintains that God is *in* everything, but that God is also outside of all things. That is, He's in the rocks, moon, you, me, your pet, your coffee, and so on. This theology matters because, according to Rohr, *everything* is divine in nature. There is no need for redemption because everything is already divine. Again, these are not mere conclusions that one draws from reading Rohr. These are explicitly stated claims that he himself makes.

But Rohr's theology is in direct conflict with an orthodox evangelical doctrine of God. We see clearly in the Bible that God is holy. He is distinctly set apart from His creation. God alone is God. The Triune God of the Bible shares His divinity with no one or no thing. We see that at its most basic level, Richard Rohr's theological teaching is contradicted by Scripture.

Multiple Incarnations, According to Rohr

Richard Rohr teaches that the first of *several* incarnations occurred at creation. According to Rohr, God entered into all of creation at the very event of creation. In support of Rohr's theology, this first incarnation provided the event that Rohr's panentheism requires in order for God to enter into all of creation. This theology should be alarming to a Bible-reading Christian. Again, we must ask, "What does the Bible teach?" And it is also helpful here to define incarnation in a way that is consistent with orthodox evangelical theology. Incarnation can be defined as the act in which the Son of God added humanity to His deity and continues to be God and man in two distinct natures and one Person. Scripture testifies that the incarnation occurred only once, and that the incarnation was exclusive to the man Jesus of Nazareth.

Very clearly, Rohr's Enneagram theology is in direct conflict with Scripture. It is not biblical.

Does Rohr even attempt to support his positions with Scripture?

Yes, but Rohr supports his points by way of parenthetical reference to biblical passages. Quite often he makes a point and follows his statement with scriptural references in parentheses. Let us all remember to not gloss over scriptural references when reading a book or listening to a sermon. Get out your Bible and see if Scripture supports the point that the author or speaker is making. In Rohr's case, his attempts to support his points with scriptural references start to break down. For example, Richard Rohr, repeatedly misapplies the biblical term "in Christ" to include all of creation. This represents Rohr's attempt to advance the concept of universal salvation. He maintains that all of creation (remember his first incarnation that supports his pan-*en*-theism?) is already divine and "in Christ." He calls this "Christification."

What does the Bible say about this term "in Christ?" Throughout the New Testament, the Bible is clear that the promise of being in Christ is an exclusive, not universal, designation made possible by Christ for His Bride. That promise of becoming a new creation and being in Christ (2 Corinthians 5:17) is reserved for those whose heart of stone has been replaced with a heart of flesh (Ezekiel 36:26-27) and who respond rightly to the gospel through repentance and faith in the Person and work of Jesus the God-Man.

You may be tempted to think "So what? What's the big deal?" Well, according to Rohr and the Enneagram authors he has influenced, man's problem is one of self-discovery. Man doesn't understand, according to Enneagram theology, that he is *already* divine in nature. He's already "in Christ." Remember the first incarnation that supported Rohr's panentheism? Don't overlook this significant point. You see, Rohr and other Enneagram authors teach that man simply needs to discover one's True Self, that is, the divine self that has existed from creation, that is masked by the False Self.

But the Bible speaks clearly and consistently about this issue of man's problem and God's solution. Man is a sinner who has chosen to reject God, and the solution that God has provided is external to man. God Himself, in the Person of Christ, is the solution. Man is not his own solution, and this disqualifies any creation of man (including the Enneagram) as being his own solution to his sin problem.

It is also quite notable that Richard Rohr rejects the notion of original sin, claiming that original sin is simply a burdensome mental construct fabricated by Augustine in the 5th century. Rohr maintains that man's separation from God exists in man's mind only. As a result, Rohr teaches that man's most pressing need is to discover his good True Self. The Enneagram's unbiblical characterization of man stands in contrast to the orthodox evangelical doctrine of the very real depraved nature of man. Original sin is a necessary component of a biblical anthropology. There is no biblical support for a doctrine that man has a good divine nature. It's simply not there.

Implications of the Enneagram's Theological Contradictions with Evangelical Christianity

What would you think if someone stood in the pulpit at your church or institution and stated (quoting Richard Rohr) "humanity has never been separate from God?" Would you be alarmed? What if someone made the claim that (again, quoting Rohr) "the only thing that separates you from God is the *thought* that you are separate from God." Would you have cause for concern, theologically speaking? What if your own pastor on any given Sunday made the claim that all of creation is divine, or he stated that there have been multiple incarnations? Would you trust anything else that came out of his mouth? These are not trick questions. Christians, and counselors who know the Scriptures, should not only reject those claims as unbiblical but also dismiss any spiritual tools or systems based on those same unbiblical statements about God and man. You cannot separate or divorce a system or tool from its theology.

Dangers of the Enneagram for the Church

At its most basic level, the Enneagram magnifies self over God. It promotes a dangerous shift in focus away from discovering the holiness of God and the sinfulness of man. And with this shift in focus comes a shift in hope away from the hope found in the truth of Scripture. Instead, the Enneagram leads people to embrace a subjective man-made solution of self-discovery instead of God-discovery. Adopters of Enneagram theology can become quite comfortable learning the system and vocabulary as they apply a self-assigned label to themselves. This provides a means for inclusion into a group. But Christians should rest in what God has provided for them, instead of the things that the world provides. You see, God has in fact provided the means for discovering God and self: The Bible. And more specifically, the gospel. And He has provided the means of legitimate, God-honoring community in the form of the Church, composed of local churches. We don't need an esoteric system or vocabulary in order to be included in God's community.

Secondly, Enneagram theology mischaracterizes man's problem as something other than rebellion against a holy God. Because it maintains that a divine True Self has existed since God indwelt all of creation at the first incarnation, Enneagram theology presents man's problem as one of mistaken identity. Enneagram theology teaches that man doesn't realize that he is already divine in nature. And according to Rohr and the Enneagram authors that he has influenced, the Enneagram is the best tool available for facilitating man's journey of self-discovery of the good True Self. But the existence of man's good True Self is a myth. It does not exist. And the Enneagram, with its own peculiar language and sense of inclusion, is a proverbial road to nowhere. It is a journey to a destination that does not exist.

Thirdly, Enneagram theology promotes a false gospel. It focuses on man's own ability to gain self-knowledge and discover his good True Self using a man-made system. If you read Richard Rohr's theological works, you'll see quite clearly that he dismisses original sin. As a result, the work of the Holy Spirit, and His power to point man to Jesus, is no longer required under Rohr's Enneagram system of self-discovery. Any means of salvation apart from the repentance of sin and saving faith in the work of the God-Man, Jesus of Nazareth, is by definition a false gospel. We see in Enneagram theology a system that propagates a false gospel.

What about people who claim to have been helped by using the Enneagram?

Our first response should be to question what drove someone to look for an identity outside of Christ. Is the person a born-again Christian? If so, we can remind them that Christ Himself has provided a new self, a new identity—in *Him*—Christ alone. Jesus Himself took on human flesh in the only incarnation recorded in human history. He did that so that the members of His Bride, the church, can be found to be "in Christ." That term "in Christ" is used throughout the New Testament and provides a picture of the glorious exchange of repentant man's *sinful identity* for the Son of God's righteous identity. God's solution to man's identity problem is a miracle, but it's not complicated. God has both defined and provided the only identity for man that is acceptable to God. That identity is exclusively in the God-Man, Jesus of Nazareth.

Also, we should challenge fellow Christians to consider what the Bible says about the idea of self. In Luke 9:23, for example, our Lord Jesus said, "If anyone would come after me, let him *deny himself* and take up his cross daily and follow me." Jesus is speaking here of putting one's self to death. He is referring to the act of denying the very existence of one's old self. This can only mean acting as if that old self does not exist. "Focus on Me," says Jesus. "I am your new identity."

Another passage on the subject of self that counselors are familiar with is Ephesians 4. In that great chapter of Scripture, the apostle Paul reminds Christ followers to put off the old self, be renewed in the spirit of your minds, and put on the new self, created in the likeness of God in true righteousness and holiness.

We should also note what the greatest commandment, Matthew 22:37-40, does *not* say about self. We should understand this passage well because it is an often-cited proof text for Christians who are looking for biblical endorsement of personality testing. What does Jesus, the Savior, say in this passage? "You shall love the Lord your God with all your heart and with all your soul and with all your mind. This is the great and first commandment. And a second is like it: You shall love your neighbor as yourself. On these *two* commandments depend all the Law and the Prophets." We see that Jesus cited *two* commandments here, not three. There is no command for us to love ourselves.

In closing, our research showed that the Enneagram's theological differences with evangelicalism are more than simple inconsistencies; they are foundational theological contradictions. The Enneagram is anti-biblical. It's theology and anthropology are in conflict with Scripture, and therefore it is an anti-Christian tool for understanding man. It leads to a non-Christian way of viewing man and understanding man's problems. This "tool" is a proverbial road to nowhere. Although the system provides its own peculiar language and sense of inclusion, it leads to a mythical destination. Man's good divine True Self does not exist.

Let us challenge pastors to look into the theology of these Enneagram authors for themselves. I would also challenge readers to evaluate Enneagram teaching using the lens of Scripture. I hope that the information presented in this brief time has provided a good start! For a more detailed evaluation of the theology and anthropology associated with the Enneagram, you can read *Enneagram Theology: Is It Christian?* (Eugene, OR: Resource Publications, 2021).

PART OF THE BIBLICAL SOLUTIONS SERIES

More
Coming
Soon

GET MORE AT:
biblicalcounseling.com/biblicalsolutions

Biblical Solutions for the Problems People Face

The Association of Certified Biblical Counselors is committed to championing the sufficiency of Scripture for the Church as she engages the problems people face, speaking the truth in love. Christians have the responsibility to bring the truth of God to bear on the problems of everyday life, and to embody that truth in a life of love.

At ACBC, we seek to strengthen the Church to speak the truth in love by providing a quality training and certification process, a global network of like-minded individuals and institutions, and a source of practical and biblical resources for the Church.

In short, we seek to bring *biblical solutions for the problems people face*, upholding that the method God has given to do this is *truth in love*.

Find all our ACBC resources at www.biblicalcounseling.com.

Mists of the Highlands

* (SCOTTISH TIME TRAVEL ROMANCE) * FAE HIGHLANDERS BOOK ONE

MIRANDA MARTIN

Contents

Get A Free Book!

Subscribe to Miranda Martin's e-mail list and get the Red Planet Dragons of Tajss prequel Dragon's Origins *PLUS* bonus freebie Ribbed For Her Pleasure!

http://www.mirandamartinromance.com/newsletter

Foreword

Dear Reader,

This is a work of fiction. While it draws from many real historical events and is set in very real historical places, I have taken more than a few artistic liberties with both events and places.

I have done my best to do justice to the beautiful country of Scotland and to do honor to the historical events that in large part inspired this story.

Many hours of research went into this story, more than I care to admit, and I have to give special thanks to my husband, James, who curated hundreds of videos and website and whose love of all things Scottish infuses this story.

I hope you enjoy it and please forgive any transgressions or mistakes which are wholly and completely my own.

Sincerely,
Miranda Martin

"Any sufficiently advanced technology is indistinguishable from magic." – Arthur C. Clarke

.

"Do not lose hold of your dreams or aspirations. For if you do, you may still exist but you have ceased to live." – Henry David Thoreau

Chapter One

SCOTLAND.

Looking out the window of the chugging train excitement makes my heartbeat faster. I've dreamed of this forever. My first memory is of Mom telling me stories of her home. She would tell her tales and I would imagine I was here, in the Highlands walking hand in hand with her.

I miss her still. The hole she left in my heart is an empty ache even after all these years. Savannah squeezes my hand, pulling my attention off the beautiful, dusk covered landscape rolling past.

"You okay?" she asks.

Savannah smiles and it's infectious, her cherubic face lights up and her flaws make her more beautiful, not less. Her straw colored, shoulder length hair catches the last ray of sun and shines. I place my hand over hers and return the squeeze.

"I'm fine," I say.

I am. Mostly. Mom's been gone for years, it's not like that wound is fresh. Gail emits a high-pitched squeal jerking our attention across the aisle to our classmates. Ryan is nuzzling her neck and she's twisting to get away.

"Stop," she barks between peals of laughter.

"Nom, nom, nom," Ryan says, continuing.

"Ahem," Professor Galmatin clears his throat as he rises from his feet and fixes a baleful glare on the young couple.

"Sorry Professor," Ryan says, sounding anything but remorseful.

I'm not jealous, really. No, it's not jealousy when I look at them, it's loneliness. Here I am, with my classmates and my best friend, but I'm alone. I don't fit in. The fact Savannah is my friend at all is something I often must remind myself is true.

I wonder, sometimes, if I'm not a charity case for her, though I know she doesn't think that way. My thoughts do. I don't fit and I don't belong. I'm the girl in a crowd of people who still feels alone. And it's okay, for the most part. I don't mind, really, but it would be nice to belong. I imagine it would anyway. I guess. I could be wrong and it's not like I'm not happy.

I've tried dating a few times, but it's never worked out. College keeps me busy anyway. My Dad worries about my lack of prospects more than I do. He had his great love and I appreciate that he wants that for me too. I guess one day it will happen. I'll find that special someone, somewhere.

The soft sway of the train rocks Gail and Ryan as they cuddle together. Ryan whispers something and Gail giggles like a school-girl and her cheeks blush to the absolutely perfect shade of pink which only makes her prettier, of course. Ryan has one arm slung casually around her shoulders and they look the perfect couple. Maybe they are each other's perfect match. Another great love story unfolding before our eyes. I hope so.

I look out the window of the train. The thick trees that crowd the track are receding, and I get my first look at Dalmally.

A thick fog lies over the sleepy village, rolling down from the surrounding highlands and off Loch Awe. The shush of waves washing onto the beach, the damp air, and the scent of fishy water mixes with the mechanical whirring and hissing of the train. The train station and the entire village looks like a place out of time.

The kind of place where myths and legends seem closer, away from the noise and rush of modern life.

The train pulls into the station, and I grab my sole suitcase from the overhead rack. I'm the first to step off the train. My foot crunches into the red rock that forms a sidewalk as sheep baa in the distance. The train hums loudly, and a cool breeze brushes across my face, carrying the faint scent of heather that mostly buries the fishy smell coming off Loch Awe.

I breathe deeply and close my eyes. I'm here, and it feels like coming home. Though I've never been here, Scotland has filled my dreams. I've studied it and fantasized about it for so long it feels more home than my actual Missouri home. I can quote almost every line of *Braveheart* and *Rob Roy* both, but getting to go to a live dig in the highlands, that's the opportunity of a lifetime. One so inviting I switched my major from pre-med to archaeology to pursue it.

Someone bumps into me, forcing me forward.

"Sorry," I mutter, turning around.

No one's there.

A chill creeps down my back.

I'd swear the train station hasn't changed in a hundred years. It's a fixed point that time passes by without touching. Down the dusk covered tracks trees and brush crowd, making a dark tunnel that fades away into nothingness. Over the trees looms the top of Beinn Donachain, the mountain that rises to the northeast of the village.

My friend Savannah finally deboards and walks over. "You're pale, are you okay?"

"Yes, sorry," I say, oddly out of sorts. "Jet lag, that's all."

The old stone walls of the train station have an ambience of age, of untold stories of the things they've witnessed, adding to my unease. I force a smile, and Savannah returns it. She drops the two bags she's carrying.

"We're here!" she exclaims, putting an arm over my shoulders and turning us in a circle.

"I know," I say.

Here, indeed, I think. I'm strangely anxious as we follow the well-maintained crushed stone walkway, flanked with cultivated potted plants. And what, exactly, am I hoping to find here? I don't even know, but I am drawn, as if this, somehow, is my destiny.

The back of my neck tingles with that sensation of being watched. I look fast but there is only a large black bird perching on the top of the wall.

As we pass under a recently painted white awning that shelters passengers from rain, supported by evenly spaced white poles with a single blue stripe, a paper taped to the farthest pole rattles in the breeze. I can't see what it says from here, but it looks almost as old as the train station.

I take in a breath of Scottish highland air. It is fresh. So fresh it makes my skin tingle and my stomach does flips. The rest of our group pushes past the two of us with some mutters about our impeding the unloading of the train.

"Okay, everyone please pay attention," Professor Galmatin says in his matter-of-fact lecture tone, gathering us around. "We're staying at the Muthu Dalmally. Please stay with your travel buddy. We'll leave for the dig site at eight a.m. local time, so don't be up late and don't forget to adjust your watches."

"Who wears a watch?" Ryan asks, flashing his jovial smile.

"Right, well, you young ones can make sure your phones are adjusted. Us old timers will handle the watches," Professor Galmatin says, rolling with the joke.

Professor Galmatin is about as far from Indiana Jones as you can get, but we all like him. He's tall and lanky with more gray than black left to his thinning hair. He has a thin, angular face but sharp, intelligent gray eyes.

"Hey, look at this!" Gail says, having wandered down the length of the train station.

She's pointing at the rustling paper attached to the pole. Everyone moves to see what she's looking at, and the moment I see it, my stomach drops. The hairs on the back of my neck and arms tingle with that sense of being watched again.

"Oh," Savannah says.

"Wow, who would think that could happen here?" Ryan says.

"I don't know," Gail says. "Dalmally, Scotland looks like a proper place for a disappearance to me. No one would expect it to happen here, of course, but isn't that what they always say?"

Her words echo in my head, ringing like the voice of a god speaking from on high. Pronouncing some fundamental truth of the universe. The ragged piece of paper dampens everyone's excitement. The smiling face of the handsome young man staring off it somehow makes it ever creepier. He's been missing for two weeks and there is a substantial reward for information leading to his whereabouts.

"Michael MacGregor," Savannah says, reading the missing teen's name. "He'd be a senior."

"Probably ran off to the city," Ryan says. "Couldn't take life in the slow lane."

"Yeah, probably," Savannah says.

"Okay, gang," Professor Galmatin says. "Enough of that. Let's get to our rooms and check in. Then we'll have dinner, and you can check out the local bars before bed."

"Bars," Ryan scoffs. "We're in Scotland. I want a pub!"

We all laugh, but as we gather our luggage and travel to our hotel, I can't forget Michael's smiling face, staring off that tattered poster. It's a dark cloud lurking behind the laughter of my group and battling with the awe of finally being in Scotland.

Checking in is painless, if a bit disappointing by how high-tech the hotel is. If I was traveling on my own, I'd find the smallest, most modest bed and breakfasts possible and only stay in them. This hotel is too touristy. It's pretty on the surface, but the slightest of inspections, and it's clear that it's a façade laid over what was once historical but not restored.

They ruined this place.

The Muthu was a 19th century hotel that was bought by overseas investors and renovated to be more modern. Now, years after the remodel, the overlay is wearing thin. The cultivated plants and flowers have a layer of dust on their leaves and cobwebs hiding in their dark recesses. The lobby furniture has scuffs and signs of wear, and the carpets need attention.

Savannah and I are sharing a room, which is much the same as everything else: overly touristy and worn. She plops down on one of the twin beds and sighs.

"Well, we're not here for the room, right?" She laughs, patting the bed.

"True," I say. "But it could be nicer."

"Of course, but we're in Scotland, and tomorrow we go to our first, real-life dig site," she says.

I put my suitcase into the small closet then take a seat on the twin bed opposite her. The mattress is serviceable, if not amazing. She's right, though. I didn't come here for the room. I came for that voice inside. The calling that, in quiet moments, takes me away to sweeping vistas, highland mountains, heather, and the mewing of Scottish long-hair cattle. All my life I've been pulled towards Scotland, but never thought I'd make it here.

I walk over to the small window and stare. On an awning that covers the entrance to the hotel is a large black bird, a raven if I'm not mistaken. It's staring at my window with a black, beady eye.

"Savannah?"

She stops unpacking her suitcases and joins me at the window. "Yeah?"

"You see that bird, right?"

She crowds in so she can see out the small, dirty window.

"Huh, it looks like it's looking right at us. Weird."

"Yeah, but is it?"

"Optical illusion," she shrugs. "Or it is and we're about to have the wildest adventure ever. Wanna know why?"

"Why?" I ask, tearing myself away from the odd bird.

"Because we're in Scotland baby!" she grabs my arms and jumps with excitement.

I jump along and we sing-song that we're in Scotland incredibly off-key I'm sure but she's right. Over our loud singing the raven screeches as it flutters right past our window. Savannah and I both jump in fear, whirling in time to see the black wings flutter right before they disappear from sight.

"Okay, that was weird," Savannah says, then we laugh it off.

Chapter Two

AFTER DINNER THAT NIGHT, we go to the hotel bar. There's a singer/guitar player for entertainment in one corner of the room who's performing for the small crowd of what looks like locals and a handful of fellow tourists.

As soon as our loose group walks through the double doors, we're given the once over by those already gathered before they return their attention to their conversations. In the far back corner, cast mostly in shadows, one man seems to pay particular attention. Although I cannot make out his face, the strangest feeling that he's staring at me causes a chill to race down my back. Savannah pulls on my arm, breaking my attention away from the stranger.

"What you drinking?" she asks.

I smile. "Beer is fine."

When I glance back to the corner, the man isn't there. I scan the room to see where he might have gone but don't see any sign of him.

Our group gets our drinks, then we take over one of the U-shaped couches while the performer does passable covers of pop hits that are ten years out of date. I'm only half-paying attention to the conversation while my thoughts wander.

"Quinn," Ryan says, jerking my attention to him. Gail has her legs tucked under herself and is leaning against him while he has one arm around her.

"Yeah?" I ask.

"You were pre-med, right?" he asks.

"I was," I say, then take a sip of my beer.

"How does a pre-med student end up on an archaeology dig?"

"How does a high school jock end up doing anything that requires higher than a 2.5 GPA?"

Savannah laughs. "Oh, burn!"

Ryan laughs too. It seems like a real laugh; I can't tell if he's embarrassed and covering or not; his brown skin with orange-red undertones makes it impossible to see if he's blushing. I doubt it, though; he's too good-natured and self-aware.

"Good one," he says. "It's rare, but occasionally, God sends perfection to Earth. You're welcome."

"Oh baby," Gail says. "You're impossible."

As she tilts her head back and they kiss, I avert my gaze, uncomfortable with the public display of affection though no one else in the room is paying attention to us.

"Now seriously, why'd you switch majors?" he asks, once he has finished.

I shrug and stare around the bar, doing my best not to squirm. I'm not in the mood to share my truth, and if I was, this isn't the way or the place I would choose to do so. Savannah knows, but she's my best friend.

"She doesn't like blood," Savannah lies, coming to my rescue. "Queasy stomach."

"Oof," Ryan says. "That would screw the pre-med, wouldn't it?"

"Yeah, who knew?" I say, thanking Savannah with my eyes for not telling the truth.

My fascination with, love of, and soul deep calling to Scotland and all things Scottish isn't something I want to share broadly. I only told her one night when we had had way too much wine. Which, as it turned out, worked in my favor since she told me about this opportunity being offered to archaeology majors.

"And what 'ave we 'ere?" asks someone with a thick Scottish accent, saving me from further interrogation. "Group of bairns getting guttered unless I miss my mark."

An old man stands with a pint in his hand, looking us over. His eyes are rheumy, his large nose red and pockmarked. His thick white eyebrows brush together and blend into the large gray and white beard that hides the majority of his face. He's wearing a kilt with green and blue patterning that I recognize as Black Watch, as well as a sheepskin vest and a black beret that barely keeps his wild, wiry gray hair out of his face.

"Evening, sir," Ryan says, untangling himself from Gail and rising to greet the local. Ryan holds out a hand, which the man takes.

"Ach, and Americans to boot." The old man grins.

"Yes, sir," Ryan says, shaking hands. "I'm Ryan Coolridge. These are my classmates."

"Classmates?" the old man says, looking us over. "Here for the wee dig in the hills, I'd wager."

"Yes, sir," Ryan says.

"Well, welcome to Dunally," he says. "I'm Gerard Campbell."

"Pleasure, sir," Ryan says, smooth as ever. "Would you care to join us?"

"For a min, I might," Gerard says.

Ryan resumes his seat, and Gail melds against him.

Gerard grabs a chair from a nearby table and sits down. "You've only arrived, I take it?"

"That's right," I say.

"Well, bairns, let me give ya a warnin', one ye be takin' right to your hearts," he says. "I'm an old man, as ye can see, been around a right long time and seen more than my fair share of what this world can offer to ya."

"You lived here long too?" Savannah asks.

"All me life, 'cept for the war, 'course," Gerard says. "Served the Queen but that's nae what's important here. When you bairns are up in the highlands, it best to keep one eye open and to be cautious."

"What are we watching out for?" Gail asks.

"The highlands is home to the fair folks," he says, looking at each of us in turn.

Something trembles in my chest, and the hairs on the back of my neck stand on end. When he locks his watery eyes onto mine, my breath catches in my chest.

"Aye, I know how you young 'uns be thinking. Crazy old man, probably half-guttered he is, you're thinking." As if to emphasize the statement, he takes a long drag on his beer. "But you take this to heart, yuins hear? When the fog lies heavy on the land, that's the Fair Queen's time, and you best be payin' your respects."

"The Fair Queen?" Savannah asks.

"Oh, aye," Gerard says.

"I'm sorry," Savannah says, leaning forward with her arms on her elbow.

The musty smell of the room grows stronger, mixing strangely with the old man smell of Gerard. My stomach flips, and for a second, I'm sure I'm going to lose the battle to keep its contents down.

"What do you mean the Fair Queen? Is that a local celebration?"

"You don't know the Fair Queen?" Gerard asks, eyes widening. "Ach, poor bairns, not raised with any eye to the past."

He leans on the table as he shakes his head. "Well, I'll tell you the story, but fair trade, buy an old man a pint?"

"Sure," Ryan agrees readily.

"Ach, well enough," Gerard says, leaning back in his chair. "The Queen of Elphame, she is the fairest of all the fair folk.

Many are the tales of her and any well-schooled bairn knows well to steer clear of her path. Do ye know the tale of Thomas the Rhymer?"

"No," I say, shifting in my seat.

"Ach, he was a laird of old who went wandering the Highlands, alone as a fool does," Gerard says. "When a highland fog rolled in, he was nae wise and did nae return to his home but indeed was turned around and more than a bit lost.

"He heard a lamb mewling and, following the sound, he came across a fair lady with a wee tup in her lap. She was calming the beast with the sound of her voice which Thomas did relate to be most beautiful.

"When poor Thomas stepped on a twig makin' a snap, she looked up and he knew this could be no mortal lass. No mortal could ever be as beautiful in form or look but she had fiery eyes, like twin flames that burned so harshly they froze him in place."

The hair on my arms raises as a chill settles over my body. In my head, I'm there, on the highlands with Thomas, seeing this unearthly beauty. Gerard's voice fades to become background to the scene playing out in my head just as it did when my Mom would tell me stories.

"'Thomas,' the beautiful lass says, knowing his name without him having spoken a word. 'Will you kill the tup or let it live?' she asks. Now about then, Thomas' belly was grumbling. He'd been hiking for a long while, and that without a bite to eat. So he says that he'd slaughter the tup and then they could eat.

"The lass nods, and with one swift motion, snaps the neck of the tup. She rises to her feet and moves to him. She and Thomas spent that night in each other's arms in the way a man and a woman are wont to do. Thomas declared his love undying for her, but she only smiled and said come the sun's light it would be but a memory.

"And in the morn', when the fog had retreated back to its hiding place and the sun was bright, he awoke alone. When he came down from the highlands to his home, his once fancy castle was no longer fancy at all. It was naught but a ruin.

"Thomas sought out a local, and when he begged to know what had happened, the good old man looked him up and down as if he was right mad. He told him that the laird of that castle was lost when he was but a lad some fifty years hence. That no one had known what happened to him and he left behind no heirs to care for it."

"How did that happen?" I ask, breathless.

"Ach, he was with the Fae Queen," Gerard says. "When the highland fog rolls in, the walls between their world and ours thins. They wander here as real as you and I, lass."

"What a fascinating story," Savannah says.

"'Tis more than a story, lass," Gerard says. "Truth be in these old tales, if you're sharp enough to learn it."

"Is that what happened to that kid?" Ryan asks.

It's as if the entire world stops on its tracks when he speaks. Gerard's bushy eyebrows pull together forming one long, wiry, gray caterpillar that partially cover his eyes. The air in the room is oppressive, making it almost impossible to draw a breath from its sudden viscousness.

"Sorry..." Ryan adds. "I didn't mean.... I wasn't..."

Ryan stumbles over words in a way I've never seen him do before.

"He didn't mean to offend," I say, jumping in to the dark and deep waters Ryan had taken us into and offering him a life preserver.

"Right, yeah," Ryan says, looking at me gratefully.

"We saw the poster at the train station," I continue. "I can't imagine the tragedy of it and how it must affect everyone here."

"Aye," Gerard says. "You cannae."

He takes a long drink from the pint in his hand.

Something moves in the corner of the room past Gregor, drawing my attention. The dark stranger is there, and though he's still shrouded by his cloak of shadow, I'm certain he's watching us. No, me.

He's watching *me*.

My heart thumps hard, and a sensation flutters in my stomach, but I push all that aside.

"We're very sorry," I say, leaning in and placing one hand on Gerard's arm.

"You're a right fine lass." Gerard nods. "It's time this ol' man was on his way. I've spun enough of a tale for one night."

"Thank you," Ryan says, rising and sticking his hand out. "And seriously, I'm sorry. My mouth runs faster than my head sometimes."

"Aye, lad," Gerard says, staring at Ryan.

I'm only half-listening, though. The shadowy stranger has most of my attention. Something glints where his eyes must be, like a cat's eyes reflecting the light.

The old man continues, "You'd be well to remember, if ya don't see the bottom, don't wade."

"Yes, sir," Ryan says agreeably, though I'd bet he has no idea what Gerard means.

The shadowy stranger lowers his head to the glass on the table in front of him. I force myself to pay attention to Gerard and my friends, but I can't help but watch the stranger in the peripheral of my vision. He looks well-built, and his eyes...the intensity of them on me...call to me.

"Thanks for the story," I say to Gerard.

"Ach, lass, thanks for the pint," Gerard says with a wink and a smile before turning and shuffling off.

"I'll be right back," I say.

"Where you going?" Savannah asks.

"Nowhere, really. Be right back," I repeat.

When I turn back to go and meet the stranger who I'm certain has had an eye on me all night, the booth he was in is empty. Again.

Quinn, a soft, whispery voice says right in my ear, and it feels like a cold breath passes over the back of my neck. Goose pimples rise on my arms.

Shivering, I turn but no one is there. Same as what happened at the train station.

I hope my dream trip to Scotland isn't turning into a nightmare.

Chapter Three

THAT STRANGER. Those eyes. The things I felt. It's silly, sure, but knowing something is silly doesn't change what I'm feeling. Like my first crush in middle school. When Billy Talbott would look at me with his perfect, ice-blue eyes, I would have sworn he was staring into my soul. Tall, rich dark skin, perfect hair, and his smile... to die for. Or so I thought then, but then Cassie Russel caught his attention long before I could work up the courage to talk to him.

We have our breakfast in the hotel restaurant along with a busload of tourists that arrived last night and a small handful of locals. Every time someone enters the dining room I look. Hoping to see the mystery man from last night. Every time I'm disappointed.

"Earth to Quinn," Savannah says, weaving a forkful of haggis in front of my face.

"Huh? Oh, yeah," I say, forcing myself to quit staring at the door to the dining area.

Which forces me to watch Ryan feeding Gail a forkful of pancake with whipped cream spread over it. He 'accidentally' smears cream across her lips then slowly cleans it up with his tongue.

Blech.

"Get a room," Savannah says.

"We did," Ryan says, grinning. "But what can I say? I love this girl. Can't get enough."

"We know," Savannah and I say in unison which makes all of us laugh, lightening the mood.

We finish our meal and Professor Galmatin gathers us up for the ride to the dig site up in the Highlands. I look all around for the stranger as we leave the hotel and get into the van that will transport us but to no avail.

"Do you see that?" Savannah asks.

"Hmm?" I ask, still searching for my mystery man.

"That raven," she says, pointing. "It looks like the same one from last night. Doesn't it look like it's watching us?"

"Yeah, weird," I say, glancing at it.

The large black bird is alone on a low rock wall that makes a semi-circle to contain a garden that sits outside the dining area of the hotel. The raven opens its wings and caws but definitely seems to be watching us. Its dark feathers contrast sharply with the salmon pink walls of the hotel.

It's still sitting there as we drive away and it seems to be not watching us, but watching me. Some memory tugs but I can't put my finger on what it is. Some dimly remembered story Mom told me maybe. Right before the bird is out of sight, it takes flight.

We make small talk as we're driven up to the location of the dig. It's deep in the Highlands so we've got plenty of time to kill. I participate as much as necessary but most of my attention is on the world outside the window. The beauty of the highlands is so breathtaking all the odd events of last night become unimportant.

I'm here. I can't wait to call Dad in the morning.

When the van pulls to a stop, we're high up. The sky is the most brilliant sapphire blue, and the air is heavy with the scent of peat moss and heather. My head feels light and it's like I'm walking on air.

Stepping away from the van, I walk out onto the high grass that comes up almost to my knees and close my eyes. I'm home, in a place I've never been outside of my dreams.

"Everyone, gather your supplies and we'll walk the rest of the way to the dig," Professor Galmatin says.

I shoulder my pack as do my classmates and then we are hiking. I'm bubbly, wanting to giggle, gawk, and stare all at the same time. The air is electric. Huge fluffy clouds dot the sky and the horizon looks so far away across miles of rolling green. As we hike, climbing higher, Loch Awe comes into view. The sun glinting off the water is gorgeous.

Birds take flight, swirling in formations across the sky. The wind blows past us, carrying the heady scents of the Scottish Highlands. Rocky outcrops protrude along our path and ahead on one is a black bird pecking at the stone with a rhythmic tap-tap-tap.

"That looks exactly like the bird back at the hotel," Savannah says.

"No way," Ryan says.

"It's a raven," I say. "They all look similar."

"I know," Savannah says, "but still."

The raven doesn't fly off as we walk closer. In fact, it does seem to be watching us, tilting its head to one side. A cloud passes over, casting weird shadows on the land and for the briefest of moments, the raven's eyes turn reflective. Almost exactly like the stranger's last night.

A jagged ball of ice forms in my stomach. Only when we're almost close enough to reach out and touch it does the raven take flight with a loud fluttering of wings and a raucous caw.

"Weird birds here in Scotland," Gail says.

"All part of the experience," Professor Galmatin says with a wide grin on his face, sweeping his arm in a broad stroke that encompasses the beautiful vista.

As I take in the beauty, I have the strangest sense of déjà vu. The breeze seems to carry hints of a song that I almost recognize. A sad, lowing song that fills my heart with a deep melancholy. It whispers of love and loss but no one else seems to hear a thing. I shake my head to clear it and we continue our hike.

When we top a rise, the dig site comes into view. A half a dozen white pop-up canopies dot the mostly flat area where the archaeologists are working. It's a small crew, five people that I see, two of whom are down in a hole as deep as their waists and are handing something up to the other three.

The three take the item and carry it to long folding tables under the canopies. They talk excitedly among themselves though we're too far away to make out what they're saying. Professor Galmatin leads the way as we approach the group under the canopies.

"Hello," Professor Galmatin calls as we approach, waving.

One of the group turns and saunters towards us with an easy smile. She has shoulder length straight brown hair and dusky skin with sharp, intelligent eyes.

"Professor Galmatin and our newly minted archaeologist to be," she says, "welcome to the Highlands. I'm Abby Calhoun, Chief of this expedition. Come, let me introduce you around."

"Thank you, Abby," Professor Galmatin says. "We're all very excited to work with you."

She introduces us to the others on her team then shows us around to the work.

"This was once a part of a clan village. This was a house that dates back to the late 17th or early 18th century," she says as we walk around the edges of the dig. "Your jobs, for now, will be cataloging and observing. Once we've seen how you do with that, then we'll look at expanding duties."

"What she means, class," Professor Galmatin says with an easy smile, "is don't touch anything. Yet."

"That's pretty much it," Abby says. "Any questions?"

We look at each other but all of us were already briefed this would be the extent of our experience so no one has any. Abby thanks us for our help then she climbs down into the dig itself and Professor Galmatin guides us under the canopies.

There's a small solar station set up with enough power to run two computers which Gail and I are assigned to use. Our job is to copy the notes taken by the professionals so that there are both paper and digital copies.

Savannah and Ryan are assigned today to help in the cleaning of artifacts. A much sexier job than the one I've got but I'll probably get to do that tomorrow. Professor also told us to expect to get to try our hands out at different jobs on the site. The purpose of our trip is to give each of us hands-on experience with all aspects of the work, both the mundane and the exciting.

I don't mind the work though it is tedious. The notes are concise but exact, detailing out the timeline of the finds that they've uncovered to date.

As I type the handwritten notes on the artifacts, I imagine how each piece would have been used. What life would have been like and who might have once been the owner. What happened to them? Did they love? Have kids? Are their grandchildren several times removed still living in the area? It wouldn't be unusual; a lot of Highlander clans have lived and died without ever going far from home.

9 June
Still going through topsoil. Remnants of wood and bits of shell.
10 June
Smooth stones in a line uncovered. A wall? N. 25 E 2.5 Pictures taken. Labeling Unit 1

The notes are written in a neat print, line after line. It's fascinating, to me at least. As I work, the day slips past without notice. They've found so many fascinating things. Metal pieces that probably belonged to a gun. The hilt of a sword and more pieces of wood than you can shake a stick at, literally. Those pieces are being fitted together to figure out what they were before the passage of time rotted them to their current decayed state.

I move the rock I'm using to hold the notebook open and turn the page. The wind is strong, like a poltergeist trying to rip the pages from my hand. It takes a minute to get the rock in the right place so I can see the page I'm working on transcribing but still not lose the book to it.

My eyes burn with fatigue, so I look up from the screen. Stretching my arms over my head, I take a deep breath and let it out slowly. Only now do I realize I'm alone in the tent.

Gail and Ryan are walking hand in hand higher up the hill. The archaeologists are crouched around something over by the dig itself. Savannah and Professor Galmatin are with them. Curious, I stand and go to join them.

The sky, which was so clear and beautiful when I last paid attention, is now covered with thick rolling clouds, dark and threatening. Lightning flashes behind them as if warning of the impending storm. The wind blows harder. The clouds moving in are led by one huge cumulus that looks like the head of a raven. I shiver from more than the cool air.

"This is fascinating," Abby says, "but we need to pack up and get to shelter before this storm breaks."

"What did you find?" I ask, looking over their shoulders.

"I'm not sure," Abby says, standing up. "I've never seen a piece like it. We'll take it back to our labs and run tests on it, then we'll know more."

Lying in the dirt is a smooth stone about the length of my forearm and maybe three times as thick. The stone has clearly been worked, having an unnatural look to it, and runes are carved along its length.

Something pulses in my head. A low buzz echoes in my ears, like the static between radio stations. I kneel next to the object and reach one trembling hand towards it. When I touch it, a burst of energy erupts in the center of my head. Blinking rapidly, I swallow and shake my head to clear it.

"Everyone, pack it up. This storm is breaking soon! We need to protect the gear and finds," Abby says.

As if in response, a large, cold raindrop plops onto my extended hand. I stand up and turn reluctantly away to help with packing up the materials.

The dig site becomes a rushed bustle of activity. The expedition's vans are a hike away, left back where we also are parked so everything that can't withstand the storm has to be hauled back. Luckily, they have a utility vehicle that will carry the heavy stuff.

"This is so cool," Savannah says, as we work to load equipment onto the utility vehicle.

"Right?" I agree.

As we work, fog drifts down the mountain covering our feet. It's a heavy, thick fog unlike anything I've ever seen before. It's so intense that it looks like we're walking through a viscous, milky substance. Everyone's feet are gone, lost to the mist. The wind blows harder until I have to lean into it to keep from feeling like it's going to blow me over.

"That's it! Everyone, head for the vans," Abby calls out.

No one argues with her. We're all ready to get out of here before we get blown off the hillside. I've seen some storms in my day but this one is going to be a doozy. As a group, we follow the trail of the vehicle.

"Does this happen often?" Gail asks.

"Storms, yes," Clyde, one of the archaeologists, says. "But haven't seen a fog like this before."

The darkening storm clouds swirl over the crest of the mountain reaching across the sky. They're so heavy that the bright and cheerful day becomes an early dusk. We hike fast but the rough terrain causes us to be spread out. The wind picks up more until it's whistling around us. There's a high-pitched whining as lightning dances behind the dark clouds and thunder rumbles like ancient giants awakening.

"Quinn, stay close," Savannah says, holding out her hand.

The first rain slaps into my face with huge drops. The fog is up to our knees and rolling down the hill faster. If it keeps going, we'll be swimming in it. A raven caws. The sound reverberates off the fog. Cold chills race down my back.

"Trying," I say, feeling the burn in every muscle as I take her hand.

Lightning cracks, blinding me. The hair on my head and arms stands on end. Savannah and others yelp. I'm sure I do too, but the thunderclap drowns out the sound. I blink rapidly trying to clear my eyes but now all I see is fog.

"Quinn!"

"Abby!"

"Clyde!"

Voices call out names, but they sound distant.

"Savannah? Ryan?" I yell but their voices sound further and further away.

The world is milky white, swirling mist. Cold caresses my skin.

"Quinn."

Someone or something whispers my name in my ear. I shiver. I'm imagining things now. Fear clenches my belly. I yell but my voice seems to hit the fog as if it's a wall, the sound falling flat with no answering cries. I trip over something and fall to my hands and knees.

When I climb to my feet, the sky is gone. The ground is gone. My entire world is nothing but whiteness.

Chapter Four

EYES so wide it hurts I turn in a circle. I breathe so fast it's more like panting. My heart thumps so hard it hurts. Fear builds and I let out a wordless, primal scream.

Quinn. A breath in my ear says my name.

"What?" I ask, turning in a circle, but I can't tell where the sound came from.

I can barely see my hand in front of my face. Part of me wants to run, but where? I wrestle with my emotions, striving to be rational. Something clangs, a sound like metal hitting metal. I move towards where I think the sound originated. I'm not sure if I'm right or wrong.

"Savannah?" I yell, and the oppressive fog swirls in response. The clanging sound comes again, louder and sharper. "Abby? Ryan? Gail?"

I yell to keep hope from dying. It's not raining, yet anyway. I couldn't have been lost for more than a few minutes but it feels like I've been in this whiteness for hours. Holding my hands out in front of myself, I take careful steps, waiting to see if I contact anything, testing the ground before I put my full weight ahead.

The fog swirls with shades of gray instead of white. I feel it on my skin as if it's clinging, a lingering lover's embrace. My foot goes down too far, no resistance; I'm falling forward. Throwing my arms ahead, I brace for impact. Unfamiliar voices shout and scream, accented by the clanging metal on metal again. A boom hits my ears in a full assault of sound that leaves them ringing. I break my fall with my arms, landing in wet, tall, thick grass.

"Ouch," I exclaim, trying to roll with the fall.

"Did you see tha?" a male voice asks.

I push myself up onto my knees. I don't recognize the voice, but it must be one of the archaeologists. I've barely talked to any of them, so it's no wonder if I don't immediately identify the voice.

"'Tis a fae," another unfamiliar voice answers. "Best nae be involved."

"You're as full of shite as a paddock," the first voice says.

I stand, and a short distance away two men stare in my direction. They're not archaeologists. Both of them are dressed in filthy kilts that are so grimy I can't identify the tartan. There are dark stains on their shirts that I'm not sure is only dirt. They have several days of beard growth on dirty faces, but the worst thing is one of them has a massive sword in his hand. It's pointed at the ground but even from here it glints and looks sharp. The other guy rests his hand on the pommel of a sword strapped to his side. A lump forms in my throat as my heart hammers.

"I'm sorry, I seem to have lost my way in that fog," I say.

"Lost your way, have ya?" one of them asks, eyes narrowing.

The two of them move closer. Cold chills race down my back. I look around for my friends or the other members of the team.

There isn't a sign of anyone I recognize or know. The dig itself is gone. There's nothing but rolling grass and heather for as far as I can see. I must have wandered farther than I thought in the fog.

Maybe the dig is on the other side of that rise?

"Yeah," I say, fighting the urge in my head to run. Run where? "My friends will be looking for me."

"Your friends? Will they now?"

The man who's speaking has lighter brown hair and dark eyes. The other's hair is closer to black, but he has light colored eyes. They casually stroll closer. I step backwards, acutely aware of their larger, stronger size. Every nerve is screaming to run, get away, but that's ridiculous. My friends and the team can't be far away, so nothing bad is going to happen. These must be some locals. Who else could it be?

"Have you seen the dig? I was with the expedition."

"Dig?" Light-hair asks. "I do not ken what your referring to. Are you a fae?"

"No," I say, shaking my head.

"What is tha' you're wearing," the dark haired one asks, pointing his shiny sword at my pants.

"Jeans…" I say, looking at my legs then back at him.

"Jeans? Where are ya from?"

"French, she must be," the light-haired says. "Those French are always coming up with new fashion."

"What do ya know of French and fashion, you bloody slob," dark-hair says.

A heavy scent of unwashed body, manure, and something coppery assaults my nose as they move closer. It makes my eyes water. I wipe them clear but wish I hadn't because now I see that the sword has red splotches along its length. I drift my gaze up its wickedly sharp length. Those splotches on their hands and clothes… those aren't dirt.

No, it can't be. This is crazy. It has to be something else. Hunters. They must be hunters. That would explain it.

"I know more than ya'd think," fair haired says.

"Never 'ad a foreigner," Dark-hair says, ignoring his friend.

"I'm sorry," I say, heart thrumming like a frightened rabbit thumping its leg, I take three steps back as I talk. "I'm looking for my friends. I'll leave you alone now."

I motion with my hands, unsure if I'm trying to calm them or me. Every instinct screams to get away, that these men are dangerous. I'm moving up the side of the hill, but the thick grass tangles around my legs and makes it hard.

"Best if you give us what we want," light-hair says.

Their twisted grins and the gleam in their eyes leaves no doubt what it is they want. I swallow hard. They're coming closer.

I'm in trouble.

I shake my head. "Not happening."

I'm proud that my voice sounds steady since I'm anything but. The two men exchange a dark look then continue forward. They separate as they walk, cutting off escape routes.

This can't be happening. Maybe if I scream? Run? Run where? Scream to who? Where are my friends and the others?

The men's intentions are clear. The only question is what am I going to do about it? Fear is an ice storm in my chest but then the cold becomes clear, and a strange calm settles my nerves. In an instant, the panic is gone.

I'm not going to be a victim.

These two men are bigger than I am by far and I won't beat them in pure physicality, but I can outthink them. Somehow. I don't want to take my eyes off them so I dart glances to the sides trying to find something, anything, I can use to my advantage.

Nothing.

Icy fingers trail down my spine as no bright ideas come. My best hope is to find my group. If I'm in a group, they won't dare attack. They'll most likely run away rather than get caught. Find my group and the odds shift dramatically.

Where in the hell are they?

The men move closer and my heart pounds faster. They move further apart. They're almost within arm's reach. It's obvious they intend to capture me. I can't let that happen. If they get their hands on me, this is over. I need space. Room to move. A chance to think of something.

When their eyes dart towards each other, I turn and run. The grass is thick, too thick. Weeds catch at my legs, slowing me down, and I'm running uphill. I've barely gone ten steps before I'm panting heavily. Terror causes my stomach to flip-flop and I'm light-headed.

I glance back, praying they've given up. No such luck. They're giving chase but I've got a slight lead. Their run is slowed by the swords and equipment they're carrying.

"Oi, lass," dark-haired yells.

"Ya got nowhere to run," fair-haired calls.

Pulse pounding in my head, I try to force my legs to move faster. Ahead, over the crest of the hill, there is a clanging sound like something metal being hit hard. Is that my friends? It must be. I'm too scared to look back.

The crest is close. If I can just reach it... Tears blur my vision. I swipe my arm over my eyes. All I can think about is to run. The men yell crude comments that I barely understand as their accents get thicker. Bowing my head, I pump my arms and legs, running as fast as I can.

Beyond the crest, someone is yelling. There's no time to process what they're saying but it's followed by a scream. I reach the top and look back. They're closing. The thin veil of rationality I'm clinging to is tattered. My heart races and cold, flat-out fear batters my thoughts.

I can't stop. Whipping my head back around, I take the next step but my foot doesn't move forward. The world tilts. I throw my arms up, protecting my head as I hit the ground hard.

Air is forced out of my lungs. I tumble, head over heels. Blue sky, green grass, blue sky, green grass over and over. Behind me are the sounds of scrabbling and curses. I hit a rocky protrusion. I can't get a breath. Can't move. I'm bruised, bleeding, and in a daze, lungs seizing.

Air rushes in, burning so bad I want to cry, but there's no time. I've already been here too long. I try to move but my body refuses. Panic rises, tearing at the vestiges of calm but behind the panic is anger.

"Get up," I growl. "I'm not a victim."

I force myself to roll over onto my hands and knees then climb to my feet.

As I rise, an arm slams across my chest. I'm thrown back, losing the air I'd only just gotten. I trip over the rock and fall to the ground. I fight, blindly raging, lashing out with nails, fists, biting trying to get free.

I'm not strong enough to fight off two grown men, but I don't care. I'm not going to let them have what they want. Not without a fight. I'm going to do everything possible to protect myself.

"Ach," a man cries.

I scream.

Tears blur my vision. I scratch, kick, claw. Anything to cause harm.

"Stop." One of them gets a hold of one of my arms.

I kick for his blurry head and make contact. He curses and lets me go. I roll to the side and keep rolling, putting distance between my attackers and me.

"Colquhoun," a new voice yells, then several voices roar in unison.

"Shite," one of my attackers says.

"Kiss my arse, MacGregors," the other yells.

I leap to my feet, head spinning. I stumble, barely able to keep myself upright, wiping tears from my eyes until I can see again. My attackers back away, looking past me. I whirl to see what is scaring them, certain I've gone from the frying pan to the fire.

A handsome young man is running at me with shoulder length hair flowing behind as he bounds down the hill. He's wearing a red kilt with grin bars and light blue lines making squares, the MacGregor tartan. He has a heavy broad sword in his right hand, and he springs across the grass with the grace of a gazelle. Behind him are a dozen more men, all armed, approaching at a slower pace.

The moment he enters arm's length, I slap him before he can

grab me. My hand connects across his cheek with a loud crack that leaves my hand stinging. A perfect red imprint of my palm and fingers flares on his face. He turns his head with the force of my blow but stops approaching. He touches his face as he slowly looks back at me.

"Are ya alright?" he asks, rubbing his cheek, but not moving closer.

I pant, heart pounding, fear and adrenaline making every nerve sing. I'm stuck between fight and flight. I stare at him then past him at the group of men who stop a short distance off. None of them make any threatening moves. He only seems concerned, but I don't know if I trust that look or not.

"Are you going to hurt me?"

"Nae, m'lady," he says, swinging the large sword and sliding it into a sheath on his back. "We're here to help."

"We?" I ask, shaking as the adrenaline rush passes. I wipe my eyes with the palms of my hands and then look at his group. They appear to be a rough lot too and a little dirty but none of them seem menacing. Unlike the two who attacked me. "Are you, uh, some kind of re-enactors?"

The man frowns, then grins and shakes his head while making a snorting laugh. He looks at the other men behind him. An older big man shakes his head and shrugs. The younger man looks back at me.

"Did ya hit yuir head?" he asks.

"No, I don't think so," I say, touching my head to make sure.

"Aye, 'eads up, Duncan," one of the other men says.

Duncan and I both look at the speaker who points behind me. I turn around and my stomach drops.

Six armed men march over the ridge. At the head of them are the two who attacked me. They all have drawn blades and grim looks on their faces. The scent of unwashed clothes and bodies precedes them, strong enough to make me gag.

"Go up there," the man I slapped—Duncan, I think—says.

Before I can say anything, he grabs my shoulder and pulls me behind him. I'm not going to argue. These people must be some serious method actors. Or maybe this is a live action role play game? There was a group that played games like that on campus. I thought they used foam weapons though and these are anything but foam.

Whatever is happening, it's clear they're deeply immersed in their make-believe. All I want to do is find my fellow students and get back to the hotel, as far away from the men who attacked me as possible.

The other men with Duncan rush forward and weave around me as I climb the hill. I'm halfway up the hill when I hear metal crash against metal. Every muscle tensing, I duck and flinch. Remaining in a crouch, I run. I don't look back until I make it to the top of the hill.

The clanging rings through the air. It sounds almost like a car wreck. The men shout unintelligibly and then someone screams in pain.

Doubling over, I try to make myself as small a target as possible. The hill is steep, so I grab handfuls of grass to help pull myself up to the top. When I reach the crest at last, I drop to the ground and look back. My stomach clenches and a cold sweat covers my skin as bile rises in my throat.

This isn't a game. The smell of blood and voided bowels is all too real. The swords flash, brightly reflecting the sunlight. I watch as they bite deep into flesh. The two groups of men are fighting for their lives. I'm frozen, watching a nightmare. I can't move and if I could, where would I go?

A tight fist clenches my bowels. Is this a movie set? No. I know it's not but why are these people out here? What are they doing?

Duncan parries an incoming blow then reverses his stroke and brings it against his opponent. The blade swings up and blood sprays as the sword finds purchase. I scream and clench my eyes shut.

Terrified, I can't keep my eyes closed so I open them a slit. I have to know if I need to run. In my peripheral vision, something moves. I turn to see what it was and a fist slams into my jaw. Blackness and stars dance in my vision. I'm thrown into the air. I land hard on something. I'm left gasping.

A dark figure towers over me. I try to scream but there's not enough air. I kick and fight, but two massive hands push aside my feeble efforts and grab me.

"Help!" I manage to yelp.

He throws me over his shoulder. I bounce against his back. Another man binds my wrists frighteningly fast. Past the second man, I catch a glimpse of Duncan. He is looking up the hill towards me. His mouth opens, and he roars but I can't make out the words. He waves his sword in the air then points it up the hill even as I'm carried over the crest and lose sight of him.

Chapter Five

I POUND my fists against my captor's back. He runs along the ridge of the hill, ignoring my struggles. Every step he takes jars me; my teeth chatter and I bite my tongue. Coppery blood fills my mouth, forcing me to spit to keep from choking. I continue struggling, trying to make him to drop me. I don't care that it's ineffective. If I can only get free, I can run.

"Let me go," I yell.

"Ach, that will nae be happening. You're mine now. I'm taking ya home. I'll tame that fire."

He laughs and it's so uncaring and evil it chills my blood. I screech and pound my bound fists on his back while wildly kicking. His grip slips. I slide further over his shoulder, my hips past the tipping point.

I buck with hips and legs one more time and I'm free, tumbling to the ground. I land headfirst and stars mix with blackness. I'm sure he's not going to leave me behind. Consciousness clearing, I grab for his legs, hoping to trip him.

"She's a fighter," one of the men says with a laugh. "I like a feisty woman."

Three men close around, keeping themselves far enough away I can't kick them. I roll over to my hands and knees, eyeing them carefully. The one who had me on his shoulder rushes forward and I lunge up. I don't have a clear plan as much as a desire to hurt him as much as I possibly can.

Before I reach him, something hits me in the head. I fall back to the ground again, head throbbing and vision spinning. Blackness encroaches. I groan and try to push myself up, but I collapse. I can't see clearly but I'm aware by sound that the men surround me.

Fight, Quinn. Fight or it's going to be worse.

"Ach, there now," one of the men huffs. "Stupid MacGregor cow. You'll learn soon enough."

I'm swept off the ground and thrown over a shoulder again. My head is pounding, I'm nauseous and I can barely keep my eyes open, but I'm not dead. It's the only thing I can cling to. Hope isn't gone. Not yet.

"I'm not a MacGregor," I say.

"MacGregor or not, you're ours now. We'll break ya."

My head pounds in counterpoint to the bouncing against the back of the man carrying me. Nausea comes in waves. Do I have a concussion? It feels like I might. The symptoms drift through the haze that fills my head, and I can check several of them off.

Gritting my teeth against the pain, I resume struggling. Either I'm too weak or my captors are too wary because I don't seem to make any headway.

"Colquhoun!" a distant voice yells.

"Trade you!" one of my captors returns. "We'll take your lass for the cows you done stole!"

"Are ya calling me a thief?" a man says; I recognize Duncan's voice. "Stop and say that to my face, you cowards."

"Coward?" the man carrying me bellows.

He stops and whirls around so fast I bounce up then drop hard against him, jarring my head again.

"That's right, Thomas Colquhoun. You think I do nae know ya? You're as yellow as the sun in the sky."

"You no good son of an arse," Thomas growls.

Thomas lets go of me and I drop. I barely manage to get my arms up in time to protect my aching head. I don't have the strength to get up, so I roll to the side. The smell of fresh grass and heather fills my nose. The nausea hits so strong, I have to stop or throw up.

I lie on my back, staring up at a sky that is too blue, too perfect. This can't be happening. It's all a mistake. Or a bad dream. That must be it. A bad dream. Any minute now, I'm going to wake up and I'll be in my bed in Dalmally.

The slide of steel being drawn stops my thought and hope of it being a dream.

My bound wrists ache. The rope is rubbing them raw. I struggle to get free, and the rope seems to loosen some. If I work at it more, I might be able to get out of my bonds. Duncan yells something unintelligible that, on some level, I know is a battle cry. Is it Gaelic? It sounds Gaelic.

Run, you stupid fool. Run. This is your chance.

Right. Run. Good idea. I roll over but the nausea makes my stomach clench and I dry heave. I push myself up onto my elbows, waiting for my belly to ease. When I can raise my head, I see Duncan charging up the slope towards Thomas. He has his massive sword held upright and to one side. His long, rich brown hair flows behind him like the waves of the ocean. His stunning eyes catch the sunlight and sparkle. He's beautiful. Like a painting or a really good book cover. My heart thumps loud in my ears and my mouth is dry.

I should run. Or yell and scream. Do something. Anything, but I'm battered and bruised, and everything hurts. Besides, where do I run? I thought my friends would be on this side of the hill but here I am and there's no sign of them. My best hope is rushing towards Thomas with a drawn sword.

Duncan and Thomas close and their swords clash. The ringing of steel connecting against steel echoes in my ears as the sharp blades scrape against each other. Thomas steps backwards under the force of Duncan's assault. The rest of the men with Duncan aren't far behind him, running up with their own weapons out.

"Thomas, let's go," one of the Colquhouns says. "This isn't the time to settle old scores."

"Tha's right, Thomas," Duncan taunts. The swords the two men wield are both claymores, meant more for bashing then finesse. The long, heavy blades are deadly in the right hands and both seem to know what they're doing. "Runaway now. Go back to your momma. Let her teat suckle your wounds."

Thomas's face turns purple with rage. His mouth moves and a strangled sound comes out. They keep their faces inches apart, glaring at each other past their locked swords. In a swift motion, Thomas takes one hand off his hilt and punches Duncan in the face. Duncan stumbles back, blood running from his nose and mouth.

"Is tha' the best you've got?" Duncan asks, wiping his mouth on his sleeve. "My gramma hits harder than you."

Thomas swings his sword overhead. The blade flashes in the sun, arcing towards Duncan. Duncan moves his sword but it's too slow. He's not going to block the blow. A scream stops at the lump in my throat, then a raven caws. Out of nowhere, a black bird dives from on high, aiming right at Thomas' face.

Every man present gasps. Thomas' blade changes its arc and slams into the ground, missing Duncan by inches. The bird flaps in Thomas' face. He stumbles back, dropping the sword and throwing his arms over his face to protect his eyes.

"Witchcraft!" one of the Colquhoun men says as their group retreats.

"Damn you, Duncan," Thomas says, making the sign of the cross. "I'll see ya burn. You're making dark deals."

"Weren't me," Duncan says. "But I'd say that even God himself can't stand the sight of your ugly face."

The Colquhoun men retreat and the MacGregors let them go without giving chase. There must be some code of battle that I don't know or understand. Thomas passes by me. He glares down then turns his head and spits.

"Witch," he mutters, making a sign with his forefinger and middle finger in my direction that looks vaguely like an eye.

"At least I'm not a rapist," I say.

"You'd have loved it," Thomas says, grabbing himself, walking backwards as he waggles.

I wretch as a well-timed wave of nausea hits me.

"Here!" Duncan yells. "Off with ya before I finish what we started."

"*S Rioghal Mo Dhream*!" The men who saved me cheer.

Thomas breaks into a jog to catch up with the other Colquhouns. The group of them disappear over the rise.

I climb to my feet, trying to assess how badly I've been hurt.

"Sorry about that unpleasantness," Duncan says at my shoulder. "Are ya all right?"

I turn towards him. As I do, he pulls a knife from his belt and slices the ropes on my wrists. My arms tingle as blood flow returns. I work my fingers then rub my wrists until the tingling eases.

"I am, mostly," I say. I touch around my head but don't find any blood, which is good. "I think."

I run my hands down my legs. My jeans have a rip in the thigh, and I find more than one bruise, but nothing is broken and I'm not bleeding anywhere.

Bleeding...oh, lord.

I look at Duncan again, really seeing him. Blood coats his face and the other men have cuts too.

"Ach, that's good." His smile is open, honest, and friendly. It transforms his face, making it brighter somehow. His eyes capture my attention. I can't look away from them. They're a clear, icy blue, like the frozen waters of a crystal-clear spring. Staring into his eyes causes a fluttering sensation in my belly. "I'm Duncan. Duncan MacGregor."

I lose myself in his beautiful eyes and as my heart races one thing becomes clear. I'm in a whole different kind of trouble with Duncan.

Chapter Six

"HUH?" I ask. I must be concussed. I gently shake my head and try to pull myself together.

Say something. Answer him. Name. Right, name. My name.

"Quinn. I'm Quinn."

"Quinn," he says. My name rolls off his tongue and a shiver races down my spine. His voice is a rich baritone. I want to hear him say my name again. And again. "Lovely to meet you. Might I ask, what are ya doin' out so far?"

"I…" I trail off, not sure how to answer. I look around the empty grass, confirming as before there's not a single sign of my friends, the dig, nothing. "I was with a group…."

"A group? Not that one, I hope?"

"Not them, no." It should be around here though. I couldn't have wandered that far in the fog. Could I? "I was with a group doing a dig."

"A dig?" Duncan asks. "We're ya harvesting, peat?"

"Peat? No…"

Blood runs from his nose and out of the corners of his mouth. His nose is swelling, and it looks like it might be broken but I can't tell for sure by only looking. I latch onto his injury. It's a problem I can do something about.

"Let me see your nose," I say.

"Bah, it's nothing," Duncan says, smiling and waving a hand. Blood stains his teeth.

"Let the lass see your nose," one of the other men snorts.

"Bet that's not all she'd like to see," another says softly.

Two others laugh, and Duncan's cheeks turn a rich red. My own cheeks warm and the flush creeps down onto my neck.

"I apologize for the crudeness of my friends," he says. "They do nae know their manners."

"They're fine," I say, shaking my head. "I've certainly heard worse."

"Well, then, the men-folk you've been around are all curs," Duncan says. He exclaims as I press on either side of his nose. "Ouch."

"It's not broken," I say. "Which is good. Anyone have some cloth?"

One of the men hands me a strip of dirty cloth. I press it to the corners of Duncan's mouth and clean up the blood. As I clean him up, it becomes clear the blood is not all his. My stomach clenches but I keep it under control. I've never been particularly queasy but the intentional violence behind this blood is different somehow.

"Ach, Duncan, we need to be moving," one of the men says.

"I know, Rob," Duncan says, pushing my hand away. "You seem out of sorts yourself. If ya want to come back to our village, we 'ave a healer woman."

"Your village?" I ask. I'm left numb. I don't know where I am, where my friends are, or how to get back to Dalmally. And, more than anything, I don't want to be out here alone. Not now, probably not ever. "I need to get to Dalmally."

"Come along, Duncan," one of the men behind him says. "We need to get the cows home."

"Be right there," he says, either not hearing or ignoring my statement. "Ma'am, I do nae want to leave you out here alone. You should come with us."

"Right," I say, trembling.

The adrenaline is gone, leaving me empty in its wake. What else am I going to do? How do I get to Dalmally? How do I get home?

"Are you all..." I trail off, looking at the group of men. They're committed to their roles, but this can't be real. "Is this a game?"

Duncan frowns, his brow furrowing as his eyes narrow. I hate myself for noticing such little details. I hate myself even more because I like the way it makes him look. Thoughtful. Intelligent.

"What kind of game would it be?" he asks. "I'm nae playing a game with ya, I promise. I assure you'll be safe with us. I will nae let anything bad befall ya."

Somewhere close by, I hear a flutter of wings then a raven caws. I look around for the sources and sitting on a stone, not more than five yards away, sits the oversized black bird. Oddly, the bird seems to be watching us. Duncan looks at it too then makes the sign of the cross. The raven caws louder, as if in response to his signing.

What the devil is this about? A bird? Seriously? Is it the same one that attacked Thomas? Is a bird protecting me? I feel a twinge of regret because that wouldn't be the strangest part of my day.

"Uh, thank you," I say. "I'll need to find my friends, but I can come with you. For now."

"Right, well, it's getting late. Tomorrow I'm sure tha chief will allow us to help ya find the ones you've lost."

I force a smile despite the pain and confusion in my head. When I look behind him, the grass is splattered with red. The field is littered with unmoving bodies lying where they dropped, dead. This is real. Maybe I hit my head in the fog? I could be in a coma. How else can any of this be?

"Okay," I say. My voice quavers and I shiver.

Duncan smiles and somehow, it's as if the warmth of his smile echoes in my soul. It's that strange feeling of only just meeting someone but sensing, on some level, you've known them for a very long time. I want to trust him. More than that, I know I can.

"This is Rob." He points to the dark-haired man. His nose has obviously been broken before as there's a large lump at the bridge. He's young though with blue eyes, a rough stubble on his cheeks, and broad shoulders. He nods as Duncan introduces him.

"And that's Patrick and James," Duncan says, pointing at the other two men with him.

Now that I'm not fearful for my life, I see that they're obviously twins. Both have blonde hair pulled back into tight ponytails and youthful faces, with barely a hint of beard growing. They smile and laugh, giving a partial bow.

"M'lady," they say in unison.

"Quinn," I say, making a fumbling attempt at a curtsy, a gesture I've only seen in movies and read about in books. It's much more difficult than I would have ever suspected, and I trip on my own feet in the attempt.

"We need to move," Rob says. "Sun's getting low. We do nae wanna be out on the moors when dark falls."

Something in his tone makes the idea of being out here after dark ominous. Curiosity overwhelms my shyness and discomfort.

"Why not be out here in the dark?" I ask.

They all exchange a troubled look before Duncan answers.

"It isn't wise," Duncan says. "You do nae want to run across the fae folk."

"Fae folks? Fairies?" I ask.

The four men make the sign of the cross almost in unison.

"Aye now, ya needs watch your tongue," Rob says. "Do nae be naming names. There's power in names."

"I'm sorry," I say. "I didn't know."

I want to laugh, but they're so grim and serious it stops me. They really believe in what they're saying. Wait, it's part of their game. That must be it. Right? Their commitment to their roles though, goes beyond anything I've ever seen.

It leaves me wondering what I've gotten myself into as I follow them over the hills. Rob leads the way and Duncan stays close to my side. The tall grass smells fresh as we make our way up another hill. It isn't long before the soft lowing of cows becomes a constant and then we top a ridge. As soon as we do, there is a small herd of ten or so cows.

"Ach, there we are," Duncan says. "Let's get this Highland gold home, eh?"

"Highland gold?" I ask.

"You're nae from around here, are ya?" James asks.

"Uhm, no," I say.

Not in the slightest and I'm beginning to suspect I'm from a lot further away than even the United States.

"Ya have a funny accent," Patrick says.

"I guess I do," I say, cheeks warming.

"Don't sound quite English, tho' does it?" James asks.

"I'm not English," I agree.

"No? Where are ya from then?" Patrick asks eagerly as he moves in closer.

"I'm... uh..." I stop myself from telling the truth.

All four men are listening, though Duncan and Rob seem to be trying to appear indifferent. I don't know what's happening or where I am, but something is definitely wrong. The one thing I'm absolutely certain of is that I'm not where I'm supposed to be. If this is a game, then these men are really deep into it. Or their delusion. If it's a delusion though then what was it that I witnessed?

The blood on Duncan is real. I rub my fingertips together where some of it has dried. It flakes away just like real blood. Which means those men we've left behind are really dead, not playing a part. My stomach heaves and I gag.

"Are ya alright?" Patrick asks.

Where are my friends? How did I get here? We've walked long enough now that we should have come back across the dig site. I think? But we haven't. Are we walking the wrong way? Nothing looks familiar. It doesn't even smell the same. That fog was weird, sure, but how far could I have possibly wandered?

"Yeah," I say, after taking several deep breaths to calm my stomach and rubbing my temples to try and ease the pressure. "I must have hit my head harder than I thought. I can't seem to remember where home is."

"Ach, that's nae good, now is it?" James asks. "We'll get ya to Alesoun. She'll fix you right up, she will. She's got the Fae Queen's own touch, she does."

"James!" Patrick hisses and James' face turns deep red.

Interesting. They think their healer is fae touched but they can't talk about it. Though curiosity burns like a sun in my chest, I don't ask. I think the best thing for me to do is keep my mouth shut as much as possible.

In archaeology training, we learn to observe first. Observe, observe, observe, Professor Galmatin said repeatedly. Only after you've done that, then observed more, then at last you may begin to create theorems. Theory created before careful observation is fiction. Theory crafted from careful observation is the truth. Or as close as you can get to it, barring further observation and new data.

The men herd the cattle who seem happy to walk along at a leisurely pace. The men call and whoop when one of the herd strays too far from the path they want them on. The earthy odors of cattle, grass, and manure remind me of home. The cities in Missouri aren't like other cities. Even the biggest, Kansas City or St. Louis, are not far from open farmland. The odors are comforting in some strange way.

The sun sinks lower as we travel. I look for anything that I recognize. A landmark or even a sign of civilization, but nothing. It's odd because coming up the mountain this morning, there were all kinds of spots that caught my attention as we drove. Places I'd hoped to explore further during my stay here. I don't understand how I haven't seen any of them again.

"We're almost there," Duncan says, pointing ahead. "See that column of smoke?"

"Yes," I say.

"That's home."

Dusk stretches its long fingers over the land as we crest a ridge, their village is nestled in a dell. The village is a collection of small houses. Each house is made of stacked stone walls with thatch roofs. The houses are built in a rough circle which creates a central area. One of them is almost twice the size of the others, so I assume it must be the chief's home. A way up the hill sits another small home off by itself.

People—men, women, and children—move about between the homes and gather in the central area, working on different projects. Their conversations and laughter drifts to us. As we draw closer, I take notice that there's not a hint of technology. No one is on their phone, checking a watch, or even wearing glasses. Everyone is dressed like Duncan and the boys in roughspun.

Something flutters in my stomach. An empty void that feels as if I'm falling. Where am I?

"Ach, cows" A little boy, probably not over four or five years old, points up the path at us and yells.

Several of the villagers stop their work and move to look at our approach.

"Hoy," Rob shouts.

The villagers talk and return the shouts. Excitement buzzes in the air, electric. It causes a thrill to race down my spine and my own mood to lift despite the confusion, fear, and trauma I've suffered since coming out of the fog.

Four men jog up the lane carrying long sticks. They greet the men I'm with and then take over herding the cattle. They veer off to the left where other cows graze. I slow my pace as we enter the village. I stand to one side as Duncan and the others are greeted warmly.

An older man ducks under the low door out of the bigger

house. When he stands up, he's huge. Wide shoulders, long reddish-brown hair streaked with white. He must be well over six feet tall, a giant amongst the other men I've seen since coming out of the fog.

His face is like rough worn leather: craggy, crisscrossed with scars, giving him a distressed look that speaks to his age and life. He strides across the open area, covering the ground quickly with his long legs. He has a wide smile that shows his poorly cared for teeth.

"Ach, good job, lads," he says, throwing his arms wide. He grabs Rob and pulls him into an embrace. "That's me boy."

Rob grunts in pain.

"What happened? Did ya have a run in?"

"Colquhouns," Rob says. "We'll need to see Alesoun."

"Right," the man says, letting Rob go. He looks the group over then his gaze stops on me. "Now, who's this lass?"

"I'm Quinn," I say, taking a step forward. Nervousness rattles around inside but I push it down and hold out my hand.

"Johnne MacGregor," the man says, eyeing my extended hand. He grasps my wrist and shakes. His grip is tight, almost too tight, verging on painful. "How'd ya come to be with the lads?"

"Thomas Colquhoun," Duncan answers. "He was being inappropriate."

My cheeks flush hot and I drop my eyes to the ground, unable to meet anyone's eyes. Inappropriate is a very polite way to put it.

"She'll need to see Alesoun as well."

"Right, well, welcome to our home," Johnne says.

"Thank you," I say, feeling strangely demure watching him look me up and down with an appraising eye in my peripheral.

"You're dressed odd," he says. "You're nae Highlander, and you're nae Scottish. Where are ya from and how did ya end up here?"

Good question. How do I answer? I open my mouth, but nothing comes out, so I snap it shut. I shake my head and try to come up with a plausible answer. The truth? What is the truth? I don't know where I am or how I got here.

"I'm not, uhm, well…" I say, stalling for time.

"She hit her 'ead in the fight," Duncan says.

Relief is a rushing river cooling the flush of my skin. I glance at him and his icy-blue eyes pierce into my soul. That strange fluttering in my stomach comes again but along with it is that gnawing idea that I know him, a sense so strong it's more like déjà vu than anything else

"Ach, get her to Alesoun then," Johnne says. "I'll speak to her after she's been seen to. Good job, lads. We'll eat well this winter."

Good job? Good job on what? Stealing cows?

I wouldn't think that herding cows is anything unusual or warranting such effusion from the clan chief. Unless… One of my lessons comes back to me. Well, *Rob Roy*, actually, but it was based on real events. In the movie and from what I've read, the MacGregors were famous for stealing cattle.

Is that what they did? Was I rescued from an assault by cattle rustlers? Cattle theft… something about that I should remember. What is it? As hard as I try to remember, it won't come. This is all too strange.

I'm acutely aware of dozens of eyes staring. Children, women, and men watching their chief and me. Some of the women whisper to each other and stare with unapproving glares. I shift my weight from one foot to the other.

The women all wear rough spun dresses and the men wear kilts that are longer than the ones I'm used to, not stopping at the knee but going down to mid-calf at least. I feel incredibly out of place. It's almost as if I've gone back in time somehow. This is the most immersive reenactment I've ever heard of, for sure. No one is dressed like me. There's not a single pair of jeans in sight.

"Come," Duncan says. "Let's get you looked at."

"You need to have your wounds looked at too," I say.

"I'm fine," he says. "Nothing at all, bit of bumps and bruises."

"You need a doctor," I say.

"A what?" Duncan asks.

A nearby woman stops working the churn in her hands to stare at me wide-eyed. Other villagers stare too. Nervousness makes my heart rate fast, driving up my blood pressure and making me dizzy. Sweat beads on my forehead. These people take their immersion seriously.

The open stares, bordering on glaring, feels dangerous. Duncan waits patiently for an answer, but I'm in way over my head and floundering.

Chapter Seven

"A HEALER," I correct myself. "You need to see a healer."

"Oh, aye," Duncan says. "Your accent is very strange. You still do nae remember where you're from?"

"Uhm, no," I say, shaking my head as I bite my lip.

I hate lying to him, but I've already put my foot in my mouth too many times. I need these people's help if I'm going to get back to my friends. I can't afford to piss them off.

"Well, Alesoun will fix ya right," he says. He points the way up the slight hill to the house off by itself. "Right up there."

He takes off for it, keeping his strides short so I don't have to rush to keep up, which is thoughtful. The other villagers resume what they were doing. As we walk away there are mutters from some of the women, and I'm pretty sure at least one of them calls me a witch.

"Why is this house away from the others?" I ask, mostly to take my mind off the accusations of being a witch.

He looks around with an almost furtive glance. Only once he's satisfied no one is close enough to hear what he says, he answers.

"Alesoun is fae touched," he whispers. "Cannae 'ave her in with the God fearin' folks."

"Fae touched?" I ask, a cold chill spreading over my limbs. Obviously, it's a bad thing and I've already been asked more than once if I'm fae touched, whatever that means.

"Aye," he says. "She's got the Queen's Gift, sure enough."

"But you let her live here?" I ask.

"Well, aye, she's a fine healer, but we cannae 'ave her in the main village, now can we?"

"That sounds cruel," I say.

Duncan frowns. "Cruel? It would be cruel ta kick her out on her own. Hard to live on your own in the Highlands. First winter would be her last."

He speaks matter of fact without any apparent awareness of the cruelty in his words. They keep her around because she's useful, but not useful enough to be part of the group? This closed community isn't welcoming even of one of their own; how am I going to fit in here?

I don't have to, that's how. I'm only here long enough to find my way back to my friends. Get back to my university group and get out, that's it. Leave these folks to play their game. Or maybe it's not a game. Maybe they're like the Amish or Mennonites. That's an idea that could make sense. A group of people who have eschewed the trappings of modern society and chose to live as folks did in simpler times. It's a bit extreme, but that's my opinion. What right do I have to judge someone else's beliefs?

Still, I feel bad for this Alesoun whom I haven't even met. Forced to live on the fringes of society, no friends, no community to be a part of, but right here where she can watch it all from her door. I'm not going to change his mind before we reach the house though.

The area right in front of her house is flat, hard pounded dirt. Duncan knocks on the door. There's a shuffling sound from inside then the door swings open.

An older woman with fiery red hair, gaunt cheeks, and piercing green eyes fills the door. She purses her full lips and frowns, enhancing the deep lines of a hard lived life that's written on her face.

"Aye?" she asks.

"Blessings, Alesoun," Duncan says. "We've been a bit banged around, if ya can see to us?"

"Come in," she says, moving back inside and letting us in.

I follow Duncan into the house. Inside it is smoky, dim, and smells like shit. A fire burns in the middle of the single room. I look around in awe at the real-life example of what I've only seen in pictures in textbooks: an honest to goodness Highland dwelling. This is a living version of what the archaeology dig was hoping to excavate.

A rough table sits against the wall to the left. Drying plants line the table and hang from the walls in that area. Two chairs sit by the table, both very low to the ground. Across from the door is a cabinet. It has two open hearts cut into the doors and looks to be well built, smooth, and stained with age or chemicals, I'm not sure. On the right is a Highland bed.

I've seen a replica of one but that one didn't have the age and wear that this one shows. The beds are short boxes with doors that close, both to hold in heat and to offer some privacy while sleeping or doing other bedroom activities. Wood is a rare commodity in the Highlands, so the homes are designed for entire families to live in.

"Sit," Alesoun says to Duncan.

He sits in one of the low seats by the table. Alesoun looks him over with a critical eye, poking and prodding his face and around his nose before going to her cabinet. When she opens it, inside are neat rows of little clay pots arranged inside. She runs her finger along them then selects one out and returns to Duncan.

She takes the lid off the small pot and dips her fingers in. When she pulls them out, they're covered in a thick gel looking substance that smells of menthol. She rubs it over Duncan's cuts.

"Ach, woman," he yelps.

"Be still," Alesoun says, gripping his shoulder with her free hand. She finishes rubbing the salve on his wounds then looks him over. "You'll be fine in a day or two. How about the other lads?"

"They're fine," Duncan says, rising to his feet. He motions towards me with one hand. "But this is Quinn. Those Colquhoun bastards had her in a rough way when we came upon them. She'll need to be looked over. She hit her head in the tussle and can't recall stuff."

I force a smile when Alesoun glances at me. She gives me a deep frown as her piercing eyes look me up and down. She tsks and shakes her head, placing her hands on her hips.

"Well, then," she says, "come now. Take a seat. Let's 'ave a look at ya."

I walk over to trade places with Duncan and as we pass, our hands brush. It's only a touch, an all too brief moment, but warmth races from that point of contact up my arm and jolts my heart into a gallop. Our eyes meet and it's as if time becomes silly putty, stretching slowly as we exchange places.

"I've nae got all day," Alesoun barks, and the rubber band of time snaps.

"Sorry," I mumble, taking the seat, keeping my eyes off of him.

She presses her hands to my face, runs them down my arms, then grasps my hands. Her hands are thick with callouses and the joints are swollen with arthritis.

"You do nae look to be injured," she says at last.

"I don't think I was," I say. "Some bruises."

"Did ya hit your head?" she asks, pressing her fingers around my forehead.

"I'm, uhm, I think so," I say. "I was punched pretty hard."

"The bruise on your cheeks says as much," she says.

She puts her hands on my cheeks, pressing hard. I wince when she touches where the bruise is. She moves up to my temples. She jerks her hands away, gasping.

"What is it?" I ask.

"Nothing," she snaps, but her eyes are wide, and she's white as a sheet.

"Are ya alright?" Duncan asks, looking at Alesoun with concern.

"Fine," she says, shaking her head. "Do you nae have work to be tending?"

"Aye," Duncan says, his brow furrowing. He looks between the two of us and Alesoun's frown deepens. He crosses his arms over his chest and makes it clear he's not leaving. Alesoun turns to face him full on.

"Well?" she asks in a tone that brooks no argument.

Duncan meets her eyes for two heartbeats before he drops his gaze and his arms at the same time. He looks past Alesoun to me and smiles. "I'll be back if'n you need anything, Quinn."

"Thanks," I say, truly feeling grateful.

He hesitates at the door, looking over his shoulder. I think for a moment he may stand up to her and stay but a glare from Alesoun drives him out.

Now I'm alone with this imposing woman who's staring at me as if I'm a specimen under a microscope. She clears her throat, grabs the jar of salve she used on Duncan, and turns around to put it away.

"So," she says. "Who are ya?"

"I'm Quinn," I say.

"Right," she says, sighing. "Nae all the story though, is it?"

"I'm not sure what you mean."

"Your clothes, your accent, and..." She trails off, leaning against her cabinet. "You've got a pull to ya, I'll give ya that. Now tell me what ya know."

Her face has gone slack and her shoulders slump. She looks exhausted. Everything about her, the way she looks, the way she talks, says she knows more than she should. Truth, or enough of it to weigh her down. Of everyone, she's the only person I've met who I might be able to be honest with.

"I really don't know what's happening," I say at last. "I was separated from my friends. There was a heavy fog, so thick I couldn't see anything, and I was trying to keep up with them, but I got lost. When I stumbled out of it, I was... here."

She nods, her frown growing even deeper.

"Where did ya get those fancy pants?" she asks.

I look down at my jeans which are covered in stains and torn.

"A store?"

"Ach, a store, she says. As if. Where would this store have been? London?"

"No," I shake my head and bite my lip.

Tears swell in my eyes as my throat closes. I've held it together. All that has happened, I haven't lost my cool. This is too much though. How do I explain to her where I'm from? Or, more importantly, *when* I'm from.

"Describe the fog. In detail," she says.

I tell her what I can even though I don't see the point. It was fog. An unusually thick fog but I don't know what that has to do with anything. She is interested though, listening and asking questions that don't make any sense. Did it swirl? Was it hard to breathe? Was it cold? Hot? Did I see anyone? Did I see shapes? And the one that makes me shiver, did I hear anything? I answer all her questions the best I can and when I finish, she shakes her head.

"Where do ya think you are, lass?"

"I don't know," I say, tears falling and lips trembling. "None of this makes sense. Is this some weird game? A cult? I'm sorry, I don't belong here. I want to go home."

"Ach," she says, moving in and wrapping her arms around me.

She pulls me tight to her chest and holds me close while making shushing noises and patting my back. It's as if the dike has blown and the flood is rushing out. I'm an emotional wreck. I'm lost, was kidnapped, almost raped, and rescued by a man who I can't possibly know, but I feel like I do. She holds me until I'm spent. When I finish, her shoulder is soaked with my tears. Embarrassed, I pat at it ineffectually as I sit up and the final sobs work their way out.

"I'm sorry," I say, wiping my tears on my sleeve.

"It's fine," she says. "I know you're not from 'round here, but my question stands. Where are ya from?"

"I don't think you'd believe me," I say. "I was with a group from Dalmally."

"Ach, I know full well no one in Dalmally is dressed like you," she says, looking me over with a discerning gaze. "And, let's be honest with one another, I felt the touch of the fae on you. You're not from around here at all."

The touch of the fae? What does she mean?

"I... no..." I say. "Well, I don't know where 'here' is, but no, I'm not from Scotland. I'm visiting it for school."

"Come now, child, tell me what you do know. You were visiting Scotland? From where? Why did ya come to Scotland?"

"I was on an archaeology dig."

"A what?" she asks, her eyes widening.

"Archaeology?"

"What does that word mean?'

"It's studying ancient places and cultures."

"Ach, who would have time for doing that?"

A raven's caw splits through the room, and I jump. I look around for the bird but we're in the house, which I only now realize I've gone numb to the smells of, but there is no sign of any bird. Déjà vu comes over me. I've been here before, done this before.

Before. Before what? Before... now. Before... oh....

As the thought leads me down dark paths in my own head, I realize I've been asking the wrong question. The question isn't where I am.

"What year is it?" I ask, numbness spreading out of my chest and down my limbs.

"Year? It's the Year of Our Lord sixteen hundred and three, of course."

Chapter Eight

"WHAT!" I exclaim.

My brain stops. The next thought won't process. I stare at her face, knowing she's telling the truth but unable to accept it. There's a pressure on my chest making it hard to breathe. This can't...No way. It can't be real. Yet...

There's nothing on her face that says this is a lie. She believes what she's saying. Images dance through my mind, each one like a photograph as I see the events of the day. The battles. The death. The dead bodies.

"When do ya think you were?" Alesoun asks, calm as the day is long, as if she deals with this kind of thing all the time.

"The, uhm, the twenty-first century," I say.

"Ach, well, that's a bit of a shock to the system," she says matter-of-factly.

"You think?" I shiver then force myself to stand up. I pace the small room three times, trying to process this. "How did this happen?"

"You're fae touched," Alesoun says as if that explains everything.

"What does that even mean?" I ask.

"Ach, child, do ya nae have fae when you're from?"

"No!" I throw my hands in the air. "This is crazy. It can't be happening, not to me. Why me? How? God, what is going on?"

"Take a seat. You'll be attracting attention."

She points at the seat in front of her. I glare at the stool as if it might be the culprit that has done this to me. Numbness spreads icy fingers out from my chest and down my limbs. I drop onto the stool in front of her, unable to take a full breath. The hard packed dirt floor holds most of my attention.

How many feet have walked over it to make it this hard? I wonder inanely.

"This can't be," I mutter.

"Can it not?" she asks, as she places both hands on my shoulders and grips firmly. "When you're dealing with the Fair Folks, anything can be."

I shake my head but I'm unable to avoid looking into her eyes.

"But, how?"

"Ach, I do nae know." She shakes her head. "How does the grass grow? The wind blow? It's tha Fae. They do as they will."

I could answer her questions but then what is the point? She wouldn't believe and it doesn't bring me any closer to understanding how I got here. Or maybe that is the wrong question. Maybe I need to ask a completely different one.

"Why?" The question bursts off my tongue the moment I think of it.

"Why what, lass?"

"Why me? If I can't know how, then why? Why did this happen to me?"

"Lass, there's not knowing that either," she says, cupping my cheeks. "I feel it in ya though. You're touched, like me. You've got the fae blood in your veins, sure enough."

Her hands are impossibly warm and comforting. Almost as if they pulsate with a strange energy. Distantly, I hear the raven cawing. Or maybe I feel it. I don't know. Fae blood. Mom told me tales of changelings and other myths of the Fae, but those were stories.

One way or another, I'm here. How and why, though important questions, aren't going to help me survive. I need answers and I'm not going to find them sitting here with Alesoun. She doesn't have them. I don't know who does, but I'm going to find them and I'm going to find my way home.

Inhaling a deep breath, I hold it for a count of ten then let it out slowly. It helps to calm my thoughts and focus my mind. Alesoun sits back on her stool and watches, waiting for me to speak or argue.

"Okay," I say, trying to reach a point of acceptance no matter how crazy all of this seems. "What do I do now?"

"The village folk aren't going to be accepting of a fae touched," Alesoun says, leaning back in and speaking softly. "They're god fearin' folk and will nae look kindly on having another one of the fae folk in their midst."

I think of the distance of her house, which sets so far off from the others. Duncan had said she's fae touched too.

"You're touched," I say.

"Aye," she agrees. "I can do a bit of healin' and such. I'm useful so they let me live here, but they're not going to be welcoming of another, not if they know the truth. Worse still if they be thinking you're a witch, it will go bad for ya."

"Right." I nod. The women of the village were already muttering about that, and it was clear how well that would go over. All my study of this era also tells me that being declared a witch is the last thing in the world I want. "How do I avoid that?"

"We'll need to get ya some better clothes," Alesoun says. "Your clothes stand out like the devil's sign and calls more attention to yourself. It does ya no favors with the womenfolk anyway. It's as if you're showing off every asset god gave ya for free."

"They're jeans," I say, looking down, then stop myself from saying more.

Jeans won't be invented for, well, a lot of years and it'll be even longer before women will wear pants of any kind. Alesoun stares, waiting with one eyebrow arched.

"Aye? And?"

"Right," I say, shoulders slumping. "Do you have, uhm, something?"

"Aye, I think I've got something that will fit ya."

She goes to her bed. There's a chest I didn't notice before at the end which she opens and digs through, pulling out a pile of clothing. She holds up a dress, testing the size to my frame. Several tsking sounds later, and she helps me to change into it. I'm unfamiliar with the style and make, but it more or less fits. Once I've slipped into the dress, she picks up a needle and thread to take it in at the waist and chest. When she's done, I'm at last dressed in more period appropriate wear.

Alesoun gathers up my clothes, which are stained and tattered anyway, and throws them onto her fire. I try to cry out and stop her, but my heart sinks and I don't. Reality is hitting me. I have no idea what I'm going to do, but I do know I have to get home. Somehow. Back to my time.

Maybe I hit my head harder than I thought? Could this all be some weird coma dream?

I'm fully dressed in a multi-layer blouse and skirts, watching my clothes turn to ash. Sadness is almost overwhelming. It's all I can do to not cry. I sniffle, pushing down my emotions and trying to focus.

"Thanks," I say morosely.

"Ach, you're welcome," Alesoun says, eyeing me over. "Here, let me fix your hair for you."

She uses a wide-toothed wooden comb, jerking it through my shoulder-length hair. I yelp with each knot she comes across and roughly works out. Once she has cleared all the tangles, she twists my hair up into a tight bun. Once she's done, she comes to stand in front of me and gives me a once over. She frowns, pokes at my hair, then tugs at the blouse here and there before nodding in satisfaction.

"Well, do I fit in better?"

"Aye, you'll fit in fine," she says. "I would nae be saying nothing about when you're from, unless ya fancy being banished to the Highlands on your own."

"Right." I square my shoulders and look around the room, then once again the enormity of all of this hits me. "What am I supposed to do?"

She smiles for the first time since I've met her. It's a sad, world-weary smile but even so the kindness of it is in her eyes and written clearly on her face. She touches my shoulder.

"Survive," she says.

Such a simple word yet it lands on my ears with a weight that crushes my soul. I force a false smile onto my lips, but tears press behind my eyes and it's hard to catch my breath.

"Do nae worry, lass," Alesoun says. "I'll help as much as I can. I'm no witch, nor can I read the future, but you've got a destiny, that's for sure. The fair folk have brought ya to us and in time their reasoning will play out."

"Thank you," I say.

"I'm only doing what any good God-fearing woman would," she says. "The Lord's own grace is all."

"God-fearing? You're fae touched too. You still believe in God? Even after they've cast you out?"

"Men's judgment does nae mean I'm lost to the light of grace, now does it?"

I shake my head, confused by the contradictions but not willing to argue with the one person who knows my secret. My secret. I've never been good at keeping secrets and yet here I am, with a great big one. One that if revealed will most likely result in my being banished and on my own in the Scottish Highlands in the medieval times.

"Well, Quinn," I say in a whisper. "You wanted the authentic Scottish experience."

"You'll get tha for sure," Alesoun says. "Now we need be getting you to the chief for you're welcoming."

"Great," I say, my stomach dancing like a flock of birds assaulting my intestines. "What's a welcoming?"

Alesoun smiles. "Nothing much. You'll be introduced to the clan. Given a few rules. Welcomed and all."

"Doesn't sound too bad."

"He won't be your problem," Alesoun says darkly. "It's the women folk you need worry about. If'n they take a dislikin' to ya, or worse if they'n decide you're a witch..."

She trails off and I don't need her to finish the thought.

Great. If I slip up, say the wrong thing, look the wrong way, or pretty much any of dozens of possible mistakes, I'm screwed.

Chapter Nine

AS I FOLLOW Alesoun out the door, I'm lost in the myriad thoughts of all the things I have to make sure I don't do and the possible consequences of screwing this up.

"Hey," Duncan says.

I yelp, jumping to the side and raising my fists to defend myself.

"Oh, aye, sorry. Did nae mean to startle you."

"Well, you did," I snap.

"Aye, I see that." He suppresses his laughter but his smile and the sparkle in his eyes give the lie to his straight face. A small grin breaks through. "I do apologize."

"It's fine," I say, dropping my fists and straightening up.

Alesoun stands a couple strides ahead, watching the two of us. She walks back to her house.

"Aren't you coming along?" I ask.

"No, I do nae think so," she says. "I best stay here and tend to my herbs."

I stare at Alesoun, trying to decipher if I've done something wrong already. She doesn't seem angry or upset but I don't know her well. She smiles and nods towards Duncan.

"I'll take ya to the chief," Duncan says, offering me his arm.

I look at his arm for a long moment before stepping to him and hooking mine under and over. As my arm settles on his, that same spark that happened before repeats. Now it's more than a casual contact that quickly passes; it's a fiery heat racing through my limb towards my core.

I gasp in surprise, leaning away from him but not breaking the contact of our arms.

Duncan looks as surprised as I feel judging by how wide his eyes are and the way he stares at our arms. A crow caws, breaking the moment. The bird sits on the crest of Alesoun's house. It tilts its head, one black eye glistening. I swear it's staring at me. Which is possibly the least weird thing of the last few days, except it looks an awful lot like the same bird from my time. Did it travel too?

"Static," I say, shrugging and trying to rationalize the sensation.

"Aye," Duncan exhales. "We should nae keep the chief waiting."

He leads us down the worn path to the main village. Children laugh as they play, running around, chasing each other, and tossing homemade balls. Their laughter rings in the crystal-clear Highland air warming my heart. The pure joy they take in being alive is infectious and it brings a smile to my face.

"Duncan! Duncan!"

Three young boys race up to us.

The one in the lead of the pack has shoulder-length dark hair, big eyes, and a wide grin that shows a missing front tooth. "Lemme carry your sword."

"And why would I let you carry my sword?" Duncan asks, stopping and taking a knee so he's eye level with the boy.

"I'm gonna kill some Campbells," the boy says seriously. "They'll nae be taking our land again. Or our cows."

The boy places both hands on his hips, squares his shoulders, and stands straight and proud.

"Aye," Duncan says. "You're right, Ian. You'll be taking care of Campbells in no time. But ya need to remember something."

"What's that?" Ian asks.

"Every battle is won here first," Duncan says, tapping the boy on his forehead with two fingers. "And here second."

He taps the boy on the chest over his heart. "And every time ya have to wield your sword, you take a wound there that will stay with ya to the end of your days."

He taps the boy's chest again.

"Aye, but a warrior has to fight," Ian says.

"Aye, he does, lad. You're right, sure enough. But that doesn't mean you ever lose sight of the truth, now does it? You do nae kill for pleasure, nor fun in any way. You do that and you're no better than those Campbell dogs, are ya?"

"I'm no Campbell—I'm MacGregor!" Ian exclaims with great pride.

"That you are, lad." Duncan laughs and musses the boy's hair. "And a MacGregor is what?"

"A MacGregor is royal," Ian answers.

"Right enough," Duncan says. "We're the rightful leaders of Scotland. It's in our blood, aye? And you do nae wield power like that willy nilly. So always remember what I'm teachin' ya."

"I will," Ian says, nodding solemnly.

The other two boys with him nod as well.

"Good, now off with ya," Duncan says, rising to his feet.

The boys run off to their play and Duncan offers me his arm again.

"You're really good with them," I say.

"It's nothing," he says. "Only passing on the wisdom my own pa taught to me."

A hollow ache throbs low in my belly and my arms feel strangely empty. I've never seen a guy interact with children so well before. I don't want to make more of it than there is, but I am impressed. Duncan is objectively sexy as hell, but add to that being good with kids? Swoon worthy for sure.

As we pass by the houses and into the village, the women are in front of their homes. Some work spinning wheels, turning wool into yarn while others pluck chickens, churn butter, or mend clothes. They stop what they're doing to stare as we pass. The hairs on the back of my neck are on end and the heat in my cheeks doesn't fade.

Duncan doesn't seem to notice or if he does, he doesn't care. I wish I could not care, but I feel like the new girl walking into class for the first time. That moment when everyone is looking and silently judging you. The worst part is, guessing by their looks, all of them are finding me lacking. Lacking what, I have no idea, but it's clear in their scowls. I try smiling at the first two women we pass but that only serves to deepen their frowns. After that response, I stare straight ahead and let Duncan lead the way.

It's not a long walk, though it feels like it with all the staring and blatant suspicion. The common area at the center of the village bustles with activity. A group of men stand close to the middle. There is no grass in this area, only bare dirt where the grass has been beaten away by time and many feet. As we step past the last house and into the common area, the men turn to look. Chief Johnne steps free of the group.

"Duncan," he says. "All fixed up, lad?"

"Aye," Duncan says. "I figured you'd be wanting to welcome Quinn, formally like."

"Quinn," Johnne says, looking me up and down. "Are ya a god-fearing woman?"

My thoughts flash like a strobe light in a rave. I've never given much thought to religion of any kind. I went to Sunday school as a kid, but my parents never enforced it and after we lost Mom, Dad stopped going. I guess I don't not believe in God. I always figured there must be something more past death, but am I a god-fearing woman?

What does that even mean? God is supposed to be kind and loving, so why would I fear that? From one breath to the next, my thoughts leap while Johnne waits for my answer. The tension in the crowd increases with each passing second so I inhale deeply and nod.

"Yes, sir," I say, unsure what, if any, honorific to use in addressing him.

"Good," he says. "I'll not have anyone to bring bad luck to us. And your surname? You're nae a Colquhoun or Campbell, are ya?"

"No, sir, I'm neither of those. I'm a Chapman. Quinn Chapman."

"Chapman?" He frowns and shakes his head. "English, eh?"

I don't want to flat out lie but I also can't say where I'm really from either, so I smile which he seems to accept as an answer.

"All right, Quinn Chapman, you're welcome to our hospitality. You'll have to pull your own weight. Life in the Highlands isn't easy, unlike you're used to in England. Scotsmen aren't lazy. We work for our livings."

"Of course," I say, nodding.

"She'll need a place to stay," Duncan says. "She said she was with others but got separated. I'd like to help her find them."

That gives me a double take, jerking my attention to him. I did tell him I was with others, but after talking to Alesoun, there isn't any way we'll ever find them. I hope not, anyway. What if they are lost in time too? What if they were captured by the Colquhoun's? Something makes me certain that's not the case. What, I don't know, but I feel it deep inside that this only happened to me.

"Aye," Johnne says. "Your friends were lost too?"

"Yes," I say.

How do I stop them from looking for people they'll probably never find? I chew my lip, but I have no idea how to stop a search. I'll have to deal with that when I must. For the moment, all I can do is survive and fumble my way through this the best I can.

"We'll find them, lass," Johnne says with confidence. "If they're in the Highlands, the MacGregors will know it."

"Thank you," I say.

Johnne looks around the village. The women are gathered in a huddle off to one side. They're watching with a mix of suspicion and glares. Between the group of men and the women, the children jostle each other. The kids seem to be enjoying the excitement of a newcomer a lot more than their elders. Johnne grumbles and nods to himself.

"Alesoun will put you up," Johnne says. "Until we can find your friends. She'll have you help her around the place, though."

"Of course," I say. "Thank you."

"Never let it be said that the MacGregor's were anything less than hospitable to those in need," Johnne says a bit louder than necessary while looking at the group of women. "Off with ya now, lass. There's lots to be done.'

When I turn back towards Alesoun's place, the huddle of women glare. One of them who seems to be the de facto leader makes the sign of the cross and turns her back to me.

My stomach drops. I'm not off to a good start.

Chapter Ten

DUNCAN TOUCHES my arm and nods, indicating we should move. I follow him past the group of women and at the edge of my sight I see one of them make that symbol with her forefinger and middle finger that looks a bit like an eye. When I look directly at her, she looks away.

"Do nae mind them," Duncan says. "Come along, lemme show ya around."

"Thank you."

He leads us past the village proper and out onto the Highland hills. The sweet scent of the lush grass covered with wild growing heather fills my nose. It's a heady smell that lifts my spirits. When we're past the last of the houses and out of sight, Duncan takes my hand.

I look at my hand resting in his. Mine is much smaller than his big, tanned, and rough one. He has a strong, firm grip that is nice. It inspires confidence and speaks to his certainty. In himself and his ability to control whatever happens around him.

I smile, deciding I like holding hands with him. I'm sure it would probably get the women in the village talking. Probably not supposed to hold hands if you're a god-fearing woman.

"Ya see that ridge?" he asks, pointing up the hill where a rock outcropping sticks out like a roughhewn shelf.

"Yes," I say.

"On top of that, you can see a great patch of berries. They're good to eat, safe. If'n you fancy a treat."

"Sounds delicious."

"Aye, it is," he says, pulling me along with him.

The hill is steeper than it looks. By the time we're half-way up, I'm out of breath. He kindly slows down and lets me catch my breath before we continue.

"Sorry," I huff. "Guess I'm a bit out of shape."

"No hills in England, huh?"

I barely stop myself from correcting him on where my home is but manage to bite my tongue before I do. I smile and nod as we continue the hike up the hill. When we reach the top, he stops and turns me around by the shoulders. The view stretches out for miles. The sun is setting on the Highlands and my breath is gone for an entirely new reason.

I gasp.

The rays of light dance golden, red, and purple, receding before the encroaching shadow of night. It's the most beautiful thing I've ever seen.

"I thought ya might like it," Duncan smiles.

He stands next to me, holding my hand as dusk stretches across the land. I may have no idea how I ended up here but somehow it feels right. As if, in some way, I've always been here, in this moment. Standing here with Duncan, watching the sun drop over the Scottish Highlands. I feel as if I belong in a way that I haven't ever had before. I am comfortable.

"It is so beautiful." I exhale at last.

"Aye," Duncan says. "But it doesn't compare."

He whispers the last part so soft I'm not sure I heard it correctly. Heart pounding, I dart my eyes at him but he's staring off at the horizon. I must have misheard him. He had to have said something else.

We watch in silence as the sun continues its journey but before it goes completely out of sight Duncan shifts. He squeezes my hand and smiles.

"We best be getting back. It's nae safe to be out here after dark."

"Are there animals?" I ask as he leads the way back.

"Some," he says but it's obvious he has more on his mind than animals.

"What else?"

He frowns but doesn't look over, all his attention on picking his way down the hill.

"Duncan? What else?"

"You would nae believe me," he says. "Trust me though, it's best to nae be out after the fullness of dark settles."

I want to argue more but we're close to Alesoun's house already. If I do argue there is no doubt in my mind that our voices will carry on the clear night air to the other homes of the village. They're already looking askance at me so it's better if I don't stir more trouble. As we approach her house, the door opens. The warm orange of her fire spilling out and pushing back the darkness is welcoming.

"Ach, come on, lass," she says. "Best to nae be out after dusk."

"Good night, m'lady," Duncan says, bowing over my hand still in his.

He kisses the back of my hand. Tingles race up my arm and create a thrill in my chest and my lady bits too.

"Good night, Duncan," I mumble, attempting a partial curtsy. "Thank you for saving me today."

"It was my honor," he says, backing away.

"Off with ya now, Duncan," Alesoun says. "It's unseemly for ya to be with a lady after night's fallen."

Duncan grins mischievously. "We would nae want any unseemliness, now would we?"

His smile and the sparkle in his eyes give the lie to his words. I'm definitely having unseemly feelings and thoughts as Alesoun all but pushes me into her house and firmly shuts the door behind us.

"I've made some supper. You're welcome to a share," she says, pointing to a pot that hangs over the fire.

"Thank you," I say.

There are dishes on the small table, and I go to take a bowl. Alesoun takes up two small bowls, so tiny they look more like they belong in a toy tea set than in use for people. She goes to the pot of boiling stew and carefully fills each of the tiny bowls.

They don't hold more than a couple of dollops in each. She sets each one down on the table after she fills it then takes a cloth and wipes the sides where some of the stew spilled over. After she is done with that, she blows on each one to cool it.

I watch her work in fascination. When she's satisfied with the temperature of the stews, she picks up the two bowls, balancing one on her arm and the other in her hand. She opens the door and sets the bowls outside next to the door on a small flat rock. She stands up, leans out far enough that she can look up the hill towards the highlands, and mutters something under her breath. Then she retreats inside and reseals the door.

"What was that?" I ask.

"Ach? Do you nae care for the fair folk when you're from?"

"Uhm, no?" A surge of guilt twists my guts. I've never even heard of this as a practice. How was I to know it was a thing? "I'm afraid I don't know much about the fair folk or the practices of, uhm, taking care of them."

"Ach, what does the world come to that it spawns the likes of that?"

I don't have an answer for her, so I dip some stew and take a seat at the table. Alesoun joins me and we eat in an uncomfortable silence.

"I didn't mean to offend," I say.

"Offend? Isn't I you needs worry about offending," she says.

"I don't understand."

"Aye, you do nae. Listen, you do nae want to offend the fae folk. Especially you. They've touched ya, I don't know how it is in your place and time, but this is when and where you are. If you'n offend them, they'll make ya pay."

I swallow my mouthful of stew, forcing it past the lump in my throat and the cold knot of ice at the top of my stomach.

"Make me pay?"

"Aye, and you'll nae be knowing when it's coming. The fair ones don't work directly like that, but your luck will sure turn for the worse. That I can promise ya."

"Right."

A chill traces down my spine when I hear a raven caw agreement from outside the house.

Chapter Eleven

ALESOUN'S EXASPERATION is clear in both her voice and her body language. She stands over me with one hand on her hip and a deep frown, staring at the tangled knot of wool on the spinning wheel.

The sun has barely crested the horizon, but Alesoun and I are in front of her house where she has moved her spinning wheel out for better light and air. I haven't seen many of the men in the village this morning so they must be off on some other duties. Earlier I was trying to spot Duncan but, Alesoun called me out on looking for him, making me blush and sputter denials that I was not doing any such thing.

"If you do nae know how to spin, then can you do the mending?" Alesoun asks.

"Uhm, maybe?" Warmth flushes my face and chest. I can't meet the frustration in her eyes. I assume she means handling a needle and thread which I've never done in my life. But how hard can it be?

"Ach, do you nae have any skill at all? How did ya survive this long?" She shakes her head, closes her eyes, and takes a deep breath. "Ya can gather eggs, can't ya? Or is even tha beyond ya?"

"I think so," I say.

The judging eyes of the village women watch the two of us without even pretending to not. I feel their eyes burning into my back.

"Ya think so? Well, can ya or can't ya? I don't want ya bringing back snake eggs or some other horridness."

"Chickens, right?" I ask, looking around at the free ranging chickens wandering around the homes.

Alesoun nods.

"Where do they lay their eggs?"

Alesoun rolls her eyes and huffs. "Look round the houses. They'll be up by the walls normally and in warm spots where they'll get plenty of sun."

She hands me a basket that's made of woven branches and shoos me off to do the work. I've never gathered eggs before in my life. I, like any proper person, buy my eggs in a grocery store. I wasn't raised on a farm. I've never been far outside a city in my life. What do I know of chickens?

Still, all I can do is my best. Though the mention of snakes makes my skin crawl. Snake eggs? Ugh, gross. The image of cracking an egg and a snake falling out turns my stomach.

I hook the handle of the basket in the crook of my arm and gather up the front of the long skirt that Alesoun gave me so I won't trip, then head on my way to gather eggs. I go around her house. The grass close to the houses is kept short by the grazing cattle and the two goats that roam freely around the village.

It seems odd that they don't pen up the animals. I've driven across the Midwest often enough to have seen the long rows of fencing that kept cows off the roads and such, but I guess they don't need that here. There are no cars and no roads worthy of the name that I've seen, and where would the cattle go? Except for being thieved by a rival clan. That's pretty common from what I've studied which was reaffirmed by Thomas Colquhoun taunting Duncan. As I recall, the MacGregors were historically among the most famous of cattle thieves. I've watched *Rob Roy* enough times even though it isn't one hundred percent historically accurate.

Something white-ish catches my attention. I kneel and part some grass. Tucked into a tuft of grass lies three eggs. A giggle slips out of me as excitement tingles along my limbs. I gather the eggs and carefully place them in the basket.

I did it! I've successfully done something.

Pride fills me as I stand up. This must be the feeling of a hunter knowing he's fed his family with his skill. The first hints of confidence coming, I continue my hunt for eggs. I search around Alesoun's house then head to the next closest house. Several women are sitting in front and they don't bother trying to hide their stares as I walk down the path. Stomach fluttering, I put on a friendly smile and wave as I come closer.

"Good morning," I say.

The four women sitting on short stools frown and look at the one who appears to be the oldest. She's a larger woman. Her face is worn, wearing her years heavily. She's working a butter churn but stops at my approach. She stares, looking me up and down as if seeing me for the first time. She frowns deeply, obviously not liking what she sees. An urge to runaway surges in my thoughts and it takes all my will to continue standing in front of them smiling.

"What is it ya be wanting?" she asks. Her voice is gravelly and rough.

The other ladies with her don't speak. They watch the exchange between the two of us like they're at a tennis match. A flush spreads across my chest and rises onto my cheeks. I keep my smile firmly in place despite the embarrassment.

"I only wanted to say good morning," I say. "I'm gathering eggs for Alesoun."

"Good," the woman says. "Idle hands are the devil's play tools. Particularly wise to keep *your* hands extremely busy."

There's no missing the implication in her tone and words. This group are like the mean girls in school, a clique that you try to be nice to because everyone wants to be in, but I'm the outsider. The nerdy girl who doesn't fit in.

Which I don't. At all.

"I agree," I say, trying my best to not flee their scrutiny. I'm here; I have to make the best of it while I figure out how to get home. Be agreeable. I can't have them judge me as a witch. "Best to keep busy."

"Aye, well ya best be to it," she says, before taking up her churn and very pointedly ignoring me.

The rest of the women huddled with her look away from me almost as one. I'm clearly dismissed without even so much as a goodbye. Pressure builds in my chest and head.

I will not get angry. I will not.

"Right. Have a good day."

Not one of them responds. They don't even look up. I walk away holding my head high until I'm out of sight around the corner of the house. I grind my teeth, clench the basket tighter, and do my best to not shout my frustration.

What does it matter how they treat me? I don't belong here. I need to find my way back. That's all that matters. But it does hurt. What did I do to deserve this? I've got to find my way home. Back to my time. They don't want me here and I don't want to be here either.

"Ach, the way she acts, all right and fine." One of the women's voices reaches me from the other side of the house.

"I know," another voice says. "As if she's not what she is."

Suppressed anger is impossible to contain. The pressure in my head builds until tears burst free. I can't hold them back. I press my hands to my mouth to keep from sobbing or screaming.

"I don't know," another voice says, "she seems nice enough."

"She's a witch and ya know it," the gravelly voiced woman says. Silence follows her proclamation.

I'm shaking and I don't know if it's anger, frustration, or grief. Maybe it's all three. Furious, I dry my eyes on my sleeve. Fine.

They hate me. Maybe Alesoun will be able to help, advise me on something I can do. If they declare me a witch, if Chief Johnne believes it.... It's too terrible to contemplate.

I don't have any answers but I do have a job to do so, I resume looking for eggs. When I think I've spotted some, I kneel and move the blades of grass aside. The white eggs sparkle in the sun. I grab the first one then something hits me in my backside.

I'm thrown forward and faceplant in the grass. I yelp around a mouthful of highland grass. Before I can roll over to see what hit me, there's a braying sound and laughter.

"Are you all right?" Duncan asks, still laughing.

"No," I say, pushing up on to my knees and looking around for what hit me.

One of the goats stares imperiously. It brays again, tapping one foot on the ground. Duncan pushes the goat to one side as he passes by it. He holds out a hand to me. I take his hand and let him help me to my feet.

"She's just playing," he says. "Did she hurt ya?"

"Only my pride," I say. "Oh no, the eggs."

I held onto the basket but all but two of the eggs I've found are no longer in it. I crouch to find them, keeping the goat in my line of sight this time. Duncan crouches and helps me search. When we find the missing eggs, surprisingly, none of them are broken.

"Here you go," Duncan says, placing the last egg in the basket at the same time I'm putting one in.

Our hands brush against each other and we both stop, staring at our hands and that simple, innocent touch. He doesn't move his and I don't move mine. I don't breathe.

A loud buzz rings in my ears. A crow caws, breaking the moment and I involuntarily jerk my hand away.

Duncan pulls his hands away too. I look around, flushing as if my mom walked in on me touching myself.

"Uh, so, yeah." I stumble over words trying to cover my embarrassment.

"Right," Duncan says, looking around as if he too is embarrassed by the touch. "I thought I'd see how you're settling in. Check on ya, you know?"

"Oh, thank you," I say. "That's very kind."

Loud, braying laughter comes from the other side of the house where the women are working. Are they laughing at me? Silly, they can't see me, but the sting of their accusations and treatment is painfully raw. It stabs into my chest like a knife and tears well unbidden in my eyes.

"What's wrong?" Duncan asks, moving closer.

I shake my head, not wanting to tell him about this. It's not their fault. I'm not only a stranger, but to think of how my arrival must have seemed to them. Dressed in strange clothes, my accent something they've never heard before. Of course they don't trust me.

"Nothing," I say, sniffling. His musky scent fills the air, turning my thoughts away from the rejection. "It's fine."

"Ach, it's anything but fine, lass," he says, grabbing my hands and squeezing.

I drop my eyes away from him, afraid. A raging urge fills me with his closeness. Desire burns like a bonfire. Dirty thoughts fill my head, none of which I should act on. I'm afraid of what I might do, making it impossible to meet his eyes. Those soulful eyes might break my willpower.

"Tell me, lass. What is bothering ya?"

The laughter of the women rings out again. Loneliness and homesickness swirl inside me and overrides desire. I'm lost. Lost and alone. Duncan is so nice, caring, but I don't belong here. My throat clenches around a tight knot as a tear slides down my cheek. I shake my head, trying to hold back anymore from breaking free.

"Nothing," I say. "It's just..."

As I trail off, Duncan squeezes my hands but waits silent. It's comforting in the most basic of ways.

"They think I'm a witch."

"Ah," he says, speaking softly and thoughtfully. "Are you?"

"What?" I ask, jerking my hands out of his in shock.

He shrugs with a sheepish grin on his face. My eyes are wide, and my mouth hangs open. Not him too?

"It seems like a valid question," he says. "Considering."

"And if I am?" I ask, then snap my mouth shut as anger heats my skin.

"I'll ask ya to nae turn me into a toad," he says with a laugh.

"Well, it would serve you right if I did," I say, whirling around and moving away.

"Hey," he says.

I don't belong here. What right does he have to make fun of me? Witch. Seriously. Of course I'm a witch. What else could I possibly be?

Anger is a pounding drum in my head. I clench my hands into fists, ignoring his repeated calls. Cheeks and chest flushing, I rush away from him. I could take it from everyone else here, but not him.

Chapter Twelve

MY BUTT IS NUMB. I squirm uncomfortably on the short wooden stool which has zero padding. I straighten my back and stretch my arms, leaning against the stone walls of Alesoun's home. I swipe the sweat from my forehead on a sleeve then grab the churn again.

Stupid men. Stupid me. Stupid, stupid, stupid. Getting home. That's the focus. Why do I care what Duncan thinks?

I slam the churn handle up and down with all the force I can muster. Milk splashes through the hole, splattering across the lid. My grip on the handle slips and the churn tilts. Leaping forward, I barely manage to grab the handle and set it right before it all spills out. I mutter a curse under my breath.

"You're right awful at churning," Alesoun says.

"I know," I exclaim.

"Ach, do nae let a man worry you so, lass," Alesoun says, while inspecting the drying herbs that she has strung along the back of her home.

"I'm not," I say, shaking my head in denial then crying out in pain when a splinter stabs into my palm. As I try to pull the painful splinter out of my hand, I realize she assumed it's a man. I turn my attention to her instead. "How do you know it's a man?"

"Ach, only a man could make a lass as upset as you are."

I storm off the stool and go to the door. Stopping, I hold my hand up and inspect the splinter then try to push it out.

"It's not him. I'm not letting him bother me."

Alesoun looks over her shoulder with an arched eyebrow.

"Aye?"

"I'm not!" I run my fingers through my hair until I hit a knot I don't want to even try to work out.

Alesoun continues staring, waiting for me to agree. My finger throbs as I struggle to meet her eyes.

"It's not him." I pout but I can't hold the lie. "Well, not only him."

"Then what else is it, lass?"

I shrug, unable to meet her steady, knowing gaze.

"The other women in the village," I say. "They all but called me a witch. The one older gal told me that the devil had idle hands or something. Then Duncan asked if I was a witch. Which I'm not. What do I know of witchcraft, or spells, or whatever?"

I wave my hands in the air, but Alesoun makes the sign of the cross, reminding me how serious this subject is to her and the people of this village. How deadly this idea can be in this time where I don't belong.

I study the splinter that is still stuck, but it does seem to be moving. I press underneath it, pushing and working the skin to try and get it out.

"What do ya expect them to think, lass?" she asks. She comes over and takes my hand in hers, raising it up to inspect my palm. She makes a tsk sound then pulls a small knife from the folds of her skirt, the same one she uses to harvest herbs. I try to jerk my hand back, but her grip is surprisingly strong. "Ach, let me work."

Gritting my teeth, I look away as she presses the point of the knife into my palm. It doesn't hurt, but I really can't stand the idea. A sharp knife poking into my flesh isn't good at any time or place.

"It's not fair," I mutter, trying to push aside what she's doing to my hand.

"Fair? What 'as fair to do with anything? Try to see what they see. You're nae normal. You are odd and you were dressed in that outlandish outfit. All that before we even talk about you're fae touched. Others sense that about you, whether they know that's what they're sensing or not, they do."

"I don't even know what that means," I say. "Fae-touched? All I know is you say I am and that I ended up here. Somehow. It doesn't matter unless I can figure out how I'm supposed to get back home."

"Home," she says as a sharp sting pricks my palm. I whimper but manage to keep myself from crying out. "Right. Tha's one of the things ya need to stop saying. You're here. Live in the moment. Besides, it's nae only your strangeness that has them on edge."

"It's not? Then what is it?"

"Duncan, of course. Ya like him."

"What? No. He's nice, but that's it. I can't like him. I don't belong here."

"Ya might as well admit as much," she says. "I'm nae blind. Nor are the women of the village. Why do you think Agnes has singled ya out? She does nae want Duncan making eyes at ya."

"What, is she jealous?" I scoff. "I don't want to be mean, but isn't she a bit old for him?"

"Nae for her," Alesoun says. "But she's two daughters of her own and Duncan will make a fine provider for 'em."

"God!" I regret my choice of exclamation as Alesoun's eyes go wide and she hastily makes the sign of the cross.

"Do nae take the Lord's name in vain in my house!"

"I'm sorry," I say, remorse causing my heart to palpitate. "I didn't mean to. I'm sorry."

"Fine, but do nae do it again," she says. "You may nae be a

witch, but the way you act is like a Godless heathen at times. How do you expect the folks of this village to accept you when you act like this? Are you mocking our ways, lass?"

"No, no," I say, sorrow chilling to fear. "Please, I'm really sorry. It's a lot different here than when I come from."

We stare at each other, and I implore her forgiveness with my eyes and will. I can't lose her. She's the one ally I have. If I were to lose her, I'd be without any shelter or help. I have no idea how I'd survive out there on my own long enough to find my way home.

"Ach, I understand, if you'n do?"

"I do," I say, nodding with exaggerated enthusiasm.

Relief floods away the fear and trepidation that never seems to be far from my thoughts.

"Got it," Alesoun says, letting go of my hand. She holds up the thin, long splinter that she dug out of my palm.

"Thank you," I say, inspecting the palm of my hand. A small bit of blood wells in the palm where the splinter went in but there's no other obvious damage.

"Good. Now enough talking. There's work to be done. Did you nae say that Duncan told you where the berries grow?"

"He did," I say.

"Good, take the basket up and gather it full. We'll make a peace offering of them around the village to help smooth your welcome."

"Okay," I say. I get the basket from the shelf and head for the door. As I grab hold to open it, a thought occurs to me. "Is it safe up there?"

"Safe as anywhere, I suppose," Alesoun says. "If'n it's your time, then the Lord is going to take you."

I force a half smile against the resistance of my cheeks that want to frown at that less than comforting thought. I'm not going to argue though. I've already caused enough offense as it is.

"Right," I agree.

My stomach clenches around a hard ball of ice as I open the door and step out for what I hope won't be the last time.

Chapter Thirteen

AS I STEP through the doorway of Alesoun's home several of the village women are huddled between their houses down the path. They see me step out and almost as one they turn their backs. A fearful flutter strikes my stomach. Lovely. They never include Alesoun since they think she's fae-touched, but Alesoun doesn't let it bother her and I shouldn't either.

I take a breath of the clean air and realize how stuffy, smokey, and stinky it is inside. Being outside is a pleasure. The crispness and the smell of grass, heather, and manure is clean and unpolluted. It improves my mood. The other women may hate me but that's fine. I'll keep on keeping on, as my Dad would say when I was little.

Taking another deep breath, I force a laugh, mostly to annoy the women who are trying to shun me. Let them chew on that. Two of them glance back so I smile and wave before turning away and heading up into the highlands. They glare in return.

The walk, fresh air, and exercise are exactly what I need. As I walk, the beauty of the Highlands rolling green and rich blue sky soothes my fear. As fear recedes, I'm left with nothing but time to reflect.

I should have been nicer to Duncan. His bluntness surprised me, and it hurt. At least he was asking me to my face, unlike the women who waited until I was out of sight to talk about me. It's an admirable trait.

I like his boldness, now that I think about it. He doesn't have filters. He says what's on his mind and that's it. Take it or leave it. I don't think I've ever known anyone like that in my life. And those eyes. My heart speeds up as I picture them. The way he looks at me, as if he sees my soul. The way he smiles as if he likes what he sees.

And every time we touch.... It's magical. Is that witchcraft? Or hormones? My scientific mind comes down on the side of some kind of chemical reaction. Which does nothing to explain that weird feeling that I know him too well for someone I've only met recently. When I'm with him, it *feels* as if I've always known him. Forever. Which is impossible, right? Of course it is. But then so is walking into a heavy fog and emerging four hundred years in the past. That kind of throws the impossible to the wind.

My thoughts wander easily from one to the next as I stride through the heather and across the peat. I climb over the ridge that Duncan pointed out, but I don't see any berries or bushes like Alesoun described so I keep walking, climbing higher and higher. The highlands aren't like climbing a mountain in Colorado. It's not like any mountain range I've seen.

It's not a single line dividing the country like the Rockies or even the Appalachian Mountains. They climb one to the next with broad swaths of relatively flat land between them which is where the MacGregors and other Highland clans make their homes. Technically, I think we're still in the lower part of the highlands too. They get much steeper and craggier.

What was the nickname of the MacGregors? Oh, Children of the Mist. Right. No, that comes later. After the bad times, when the MacGregor name was outlawed.

Ahead of me rises a massive peak which I stop to admire. The rays of the sun dance on the snow caps. Three birds circle around it. They must be huge birds because they look sizable even from this distance. I drink in the beauty of my surroundings as I turn a slow circle. My chest expands and it feels as if I'm lifting out of my own body.

My smile is so wide it hurts but I'm here to do a job and I'd best be to it, so I turn my attention to finding berries. When I turn back to resume my climb, there's a raven sitting on a rock not a dozen feet away.

"Hello," I say. Crazy, maybe, but it looks like the same one that I keep seeing. "It sure seems you're following me."

The raven tilts its head in an almost inquisitive look. It's pure black eyes sparkle and its beak is part way open. I stare at it for a long moment while feeling something. Something I can't put my finger on. It's not so much a feeling as it is a calling. A memory? A sense of having lost something or not remembering something I should remember.

Shaking my head to clear it, I resume walking. The bird will do what the bird is going to do. After all, it's a bird. Anything else is me projecting onto it. I don't need to engage in any anthropomorphism; My life is already weird enough.

As I walk closer, the raven doesn't move. Strange, but so is everything else and that barely ranks on the scale of odd occurrences. I slow my steps but keep walking until I'm almost within an arm's reach. The raven caws loudly. So loud it almost hurts my ears. It flutters its wings, hopping from one foot to the other. I stop approaching when it doesn't take off in flight.

"You're a strange bird," I say. "Are you not scared of me? I'm much bigger than you. I'm warning you—you'd best be on your way. Shoo."

I make small motions with my hands trying to shoo the bird away while not wanting to engage it too much. The last thing I need is to have a battle with a bird. I saw what that bird did to

Thomas when he was fighting with Duncan. I don't want raven claws on my face. The raven caws, wings open wide, and prances about on the stone.

"Fine," I say, taking a step back.

After I take two more, it settles down, stopping its noise and folding its wings closed. The bird and I stare at each other and that strange tingling feeling continues at the edges of my awareness. It feels like something I should know or did know. Like trying to remember something that is right there, on the tip of my tongue. Scowling, I try to figure it out. As I do, the raven bobs its head up and down as if encouraging me.

"Stop it, Quinn," I say out loud, mostly to hear any sound besides the soft blow of the wind and the noise the raven is making. "It's not human. It's a bird. A freaky bird, yes, but a bird all the same."

The raven caws and opens its wings wide as if protesting my assessment. I rub my forehead. I'm losing it for sure. Maybe that's what has been going on this entire time. I've gone off the deep end. This is all some fantasy purely in my head. If it is, though, it sure feels real. Too real.

I can't force the sensation to coalesce into anything more and now I feel foolish. Shaking my head, I throw my hands up in the air. This is ridiculous.

"You win, bird. You win."

I turn my back on the raven and stride off in a new direction. As I do, the hairs on the back of my neck stand on end and my shoulder muscles knot. I feel like I need to be ready to duck an attack. Goose pimples raise on my arms. I roll my shoulders trying to ease the pressure, but it doesn't help. I try to ignore it, but the sensation grows stronger. At last, I give up and dare to look back over my shoulder.

The raven is gone. As if it was never there in the first place. Where it was is a thick fog rolling down from the mountain. Fear flutters through my soul, the thrumming wings of a hummingbird pressing against my sanity.

"Oh, god," I mutter.

Chapter Fourteen

FOG. Like the fog that ended up with me here. Could it have come to take me home? Is my adventure about to end? Or will I be dumped in some other place and time? Each possibility drifts through my thoughts but then the worst of them all occurs to me.

What if nothing happens at all? What if this is it? I'm stuck here, lost in time to live out the rest of my days.

My heart speeds up as cold sweat trickles between my breasts and down my back. Berries or not, I need to get back to Alesoun's home. I whirl away from the incoming fog. As I do, something dark flashes in the edge of the fog. Dark and human shaped. I turn back to confront the blur but there's nothing there. It must have been some kind of artifact of light reflecting oddly off the fog.

Fear settles on me for real. Chills race along my limbs and my breath speeds up to match the racing of my heart. I know better than to run. The ground up here is treacherous with unexpected holes hidden by the grass, any one of which could break an ankle. There are plenty of rocks to trip me up but danger or no, I'm not hanging out here and waiting. I stride down the hill. I'm off the path I took coming up and looking around I can't spot it.

"Good job," I mutter to myself. My getting lost skill has leveled up.

Something moves in my peripheral. I jerk away from it while looking towards it. A man stands a short way off, staring at me. The sunlight hits him from behind, casting him in dark shadow. The fog is thick on the ground around him coming up to his calf. I can't see his eyes, but he seems to be staring at me.

Memories of my treatment at the hands of the Colquhouns and their threats are too fresh to risk confronting a stranger alone. This is far from an enlightened age for women's rights and no matter how liberal I might consider myself to be, I'm also not an idiot. Armed or not, a man will be bigger and stronger than I am. I won't be able to fight him off if he wants to harm me or worse.

Throwing caution to the wind, I break into a run. I glance over my shoulder to look for any pursuit and he's gone. Was he really there? Is my fear causing me to see things or make more out of things than they are? Maybe it was a rock. Or a reflection. A casting of light. Something?

I don't know but I'm scared. Scared enough I'm not going to hang out here and wait to see if it was a figment of my imagination. I force myself to stop running though, because without a imminent threat, the danger that the ground presents is real.

Slowing to a walk, I work to catch my breath while figuring out the way back to the village. I know I need to go down, so I keep moving in that direction but the fog rolling in is covering all the landmarks I made note of on my way up.

"I'm not lost. I'm not lost," I mutter to reassure myself.

I swivel my head trying to spot things I recognize. Anything to orient myself to the way back. Once again, I spot a dark figure in my peripheral vision but this time, he's closer. As if he is popping up out of the fog itself. I yelp, a loud squeak that is a long way from dignified, but this isn't the time for dignity. It's time for survival.

I burst into a run. I know I'm losing it when the wind feels like it's pushing against me. The fog is over my feet, obscuring the ground. I race faster but it feels like the fog is slowing me down. It's all in my head; it has to be. It's fear. All of this is fear, that's all. I have to get to the village or close enough that I can yell. If they hear me, they'll send help.

Duncan will come. He'll protect me.

I glance over my shoulder and the dark figure is closer. There's no doubt I see him. As I open my mouth to yell at him, I trip.

I'm thrown forward, wrenching my back and neck. I throw my arms up barely in time to break my fall. I hit the ground hard. My teeth rattle painfully but I manage to avoid hitting my head. There's no time to be lying here moaning, so I leap to my feet.

"Are you all right?" The voice is a rich baritone that resounds through me, echoing in my core.

"I'll be fine," I say, turning to face the stranger and taking a step back to keep some distance between us.

He's dark and in what is becoming commonplace, familiar. Shadows seem to cling to him, making it hard to discern the details of his appearance. He has thick, curly hair that looks like it has a mind of its own, some pieces sticking out oddly while still managing to look good. He has a youthful appearance, as if he's somehow untouched by the world around him. Almost as if he's not really a part of it but only an observer. As if he's too odd, too different to be affected by reality.

"Good," he says, not smiling but not frowning. His eyes are deep brown with emerald flecks, and they feel like they look past me, as if I'm not really here either. "I need you, Quinn."

My heart leaps into my throat. I blink, slowly, placing my hands on my hips. I work moisture back into my mouth while we stare at each other.

"How do you know my name?"

"I know everything about you."

"Nice. Cryptic and creepy. Is that what you're going for? Highland creeper? Really?"

He blinks which seems to happen in slow motion, as if his eyelids move on their own bandwidth of time, slowly closing without any care in the world, meeting, then slowly parting as they return to open. He purses his lips and tilts his head slightly to the left.

"Wrong question."

"Wrong question? What?" I frown, mind racing. "Wait. You know something about how I'm here!"

The corners of his lips flirt with becoming a smile but the effort of moving up proves too much for them, leaving his face grim.

"This is your destiny," he says.

"My destiny? Right. I'll get right on that. Oh, wait, I don't have any clue what you're talking about!"

He arches an eyebrow as anger carries me away.

"Who are you?"

"Wrong question, again," he says, his face seeming to cloud over as his eyes narrow. "We don't have time for this. Think."

I stop, eyes widening, and anger burns into rage.

"Oh, you did not," I say, my voice soft. "You did not just tell me to think."

"Quinn," he says, raising his hands between us, making soothing motions.

"No," I say, pointing my finger at him. "You don't get to *Quinn* me. I don't know who you are or how you know my name."

"You do know me," he insists, taking a step back. He glances over his shoulder. I peek too but I don't know what it is he is looking at as there's nothing but blank fog. When he turns back, his frown deepens and his eyes flash as he grimaces. "We don't have time for this."

It feels like his words echo in my head, reverberating, repeating back on themselves. They're trying to coalesce, form something, tugging at memory. Déjà vu drifts through but there's nothing for it to latch on to, leaving me with a sense of this being vaguely familiar. As if he's a grade school classmate whom I've mostly forgotten before meeting again twenty years later.

The fog thickens, rising to my calves. A storm is rolling in with clouds so dark they shade from bruised purple to almost black. Lightning flashes behind them and if I know any one thing for sure, it's that I don't want to be out here in the open when that storm breaks. The wind blows harder, pulling at the dark cloak the stranger wears.

"Right," I say. "No time. I'm leaving."

I turn and as I take a step, he grabs my shoulder with a grip like a vise, spinning me around to face him.

"Listen!"

"Don't." I jerk free of his grip. "Don't ever grab me."

I all but growl the words, and he raises his hands in surrender.

"I'm sorry," he says, shaking his head, "but you must listen."

"I'm listening."

"You have a destiny. You don't know it, or don't recall it," he says. "You have to realize who you are, your true self."

"You're insane," I say.

He looks at the approaching storm again and this time when he turns back, I would swear the look on his face is one of fear.

"In seven days, the moon will be full," he says and points off to the west. "Over there, you see that standing stone? Meet me there before the midnight hour."

"Why should I?"

"I'll help you find your way," he says cryptically.

He whirls away, his cloak flying up and across my vision. I raise my arms to protect my face and by the time I blink and drop them he's gone. I turn a full circle looking for him but there's not a sign of him. Somewhere, a bird caws. The only sound besides the whistling wind of the approaching storm.

My stomach tightens into a hard knot. I grip the empty basket tight to my chest, turn, and run for the village.

Chapter Fifteen

WHO IS HE? The same question that kept me from sleeping last night still burns this morning.

I thrust the stick into the butter churn with more force than is necessary, using my frustration and low boiling anger to push past the burning sensation in my arms. I stop and wipe the sweat off my forehead with my sleeve. Damn, this is a lot of work. Churning is one of the few tasks Alesoun has put me on that I've been successful at. Which isn't saying much since it's mostly shoving a stick in and out of a barrel.

"Do nae let it rest. You'll ruin it," Alesoun says from inside the house.

"Right," I sigh, resuming my work.

Down the path from her house, the group of women cast dark glances in my direction. When they laugh, my cheeks warm. I'm sure they're still talking about me. I'm the most popular talking point in the village, after all. I attack the butter churn, pouring my anger into every thrust.

This is all stupid. A grand destiny? Me? Right. I'm not special; I'm lost. I'm out of my time and out of place. I don't belong here.

What of Duncan? one part of my mind asks the other part.

What about him? comes the snap response. *I don't belong here. Somehow, I have to get back home. Back to my time. And what then? What of this spark of romance, if that's even what it is? Nothing, that's what. Big, fat nothing. How can I possibly have a relationship with a man who's four hundred years before I'll be born? That's a freaking bust.*

"If ya keep working that churn that hard you're going to break it," Duncan says, startling me.

"Ah!" I jump backwards off the low stool.

The butter churn tilts precariously, falling away. Scrambling, I try to grab the handle but miss. Duncan moves so fast it's almost preternatural. He captures the runaway churn and returns it upright. He smiles and damn it if my heart doesn't melt. His smile is the sun breaking through the gray clouds of doubt.

"I'm sorry, did nae mean to startle ya," he says.

The wind tugs at his hair, pulling random strands here and there as if they're waving with a mind of their own. When I meet his eyes, my mouth goes dry and heart palpitations rattle inside my chest.

I compare him to the dark stranger I met on the moors. Duncan's icy blue eyes versus the deep brown. Light versus dark.

My God, Quinn, knock it off. I can't fall for either of these guys!

"Well, you did," I say, which comes out sharper and harsher than I want. Regret blossoms like a spark catching fire. I open my mouth to apologize but he speaks before I can.

"Ach, your tongue is razor sharp today."

"My tongue?" I ask, one hand on my hips. "Are you serious?"

He furrows his brow. "I did nae come to argue with ya."

"No? Then why did you come?"

I see the group of women past him are watching our exchange with clear disapproval. Their words from earlier in the week echo in my head. They don't want me flirting with Duncan. I shouldn't be flirting with him anyway. Not because they don't want me too, but because I want to get back home. Therefore, I have no business holding his interest. It's not fair to him or the villagers. Maybe if I push him away, they'll be nicer?

"I was gonna ask you to take a walk with me," he says.

"You were, were you? You think I don't have work to do?"

"Well, of course you do," he says, as his shoulders slump. "But I thought it would be nice. Give ya a break."

"Give the lad a break," Alesoun says, appearing in the doorway. "Go on, take a walk with him."

I glare at her. She's not helping in the slightest. Of course I want to take a walk with him. I like him, but that's not the point. What right do I have to like him? I don't belong here. I was trying to be a good person and push him away. Now Alesoun has blown holes all through my best excuse, which was her. I close my eyes and swallow hard, trying to force down the clog of emotions sticking in my throat.

You have a destiny. You don't know it or don't recall it. The stranger's voice echoes in my head as it has over and over since I met him.

A destiny. I've never believed in destiny. Or fate. Or kismet. I couldn't even say I really believed in God or having faith or pretty much anything I couldn't touch. Despite my lack of faith or belief, I'm here. In this impossible place, in an impossible time, and it has to mean *something,* doesn't it? Is that something destiny? What if Duncan is that destiny?

He could be my Highland prince, meant to sweep me off my feet and carry me across the heather... Oh god, stop.

"I'm... I'm sorry," I say. I shake my head to try and clear it of my nonsensical fantasies, but I can't look up or meet his eyes.

"It's fine," he says. When I don't meet his eyes, but continue staring at the butter churn he adds, "Really."

Does he have to be so nice? Understanding and forgiving? Does he have any bad traits? Could this possibly be any harder?

"Thanks," I say, darting my eyes up to his face. Man, I really like his face. Strong jaw, full lips on a wide mouth, and those eyes. I suppress a shiver and return my gaze to the churn. "What about the butter?"

"I'll take care of it," Alesoun says, grabbing the handle of the churn and setting to work without another word.

I wipe my sweaty hands on my apron. As I untie the apron, I see the women are shooting death glares and my stomach sinks. I can't do anything about them, so I turn away. Let them. They're probably going to hate me no matter what I do anyway, so let them hate.

"Where do you want to go?" I ask Duncan.

"Come along," he says, offering his arm.

I take his arm, resting my hand on his forearm. The moment my hand touches him, I get the same sensation that is becoming familiar. A tugging of something half-remembered. Something I should know is mixing with a sense of rightness. As if his arm, this time, this moment is *exactly* where I'm supposed to be. That sense is deeper than any déjà vu. It's less a momentary kind of remembered familiarity. It's bone deep, in my soul I suppose. A true sense that I've known this man for so much longer than there is any way I possibly could have.

He leads me along and we walk away from the village in a different direction than I've gone before. We go past the cows that are grazing on this side of the village today. They seem to work their way up and down the grass of the highlands.

Neither of us talk, maintaining a silence that is too easy, too comfortable for people who don't really know each other. The kind of silence I imagine long-term lovers can fall into.

"It's beautiful here," I say, breaking the silence solely because it's too comfortable.

I really can't fall for him. Or let him fall for me. I'm going to go home. What kind of person would I be if I did? A trollop? I stop myself from giggling at the word.

"Aye," he says. "What is it like where you're from?"

I glance sidelong at him. I chew my lip trying to formulate an answer he'll understand. The new world, as they'd call it now, is barely a blip on the map and where I'm actually from doesn't exist. Won't for hundreds of years. I have to be careful, or I'll be labeled a witch for sure.

"Not this nice," I say at last.

"Well," he says with a huff, "how can it be?"

"What do you mean?"

"I don't rightly assume that any place that had you in it could possibly compare to your own beauty. It would be put to shame in comparison, no matter how nice it was."

Heat rushes to my cheeks and other parts of me. Parts that have no business warming, not when I know I can't let this go on. I can't act. I won't kiss him. I won't. Nope, not going to do it.

Be a good girl.

"You are a ridiculous man," I say, attempting to deflect his attention.

"Perhaps," he says, before falling silent.

We walk on and as we do, I am so taken with my surroundings I forget that I'd decided to not let the silence between us go on. The sweeping green dotted with purple heather stretching out until it meets the brilliant blue of the sky is breathtaking.

"I'd hoped to steal some time with ya," he says. "Before I'll be gone for a bit."

Gone? It's a good thing if he'll be gone. Best way to avoid temptation is to remove yourself from it. But if it's good, then why has my stomach dropped to the ground?

"You're leaving?" I try to sound casual, barely interested, but the strain is clear in my voice if he has ears at all.

"Aye. We'll be off to get some cattle."

Chills pass over me and a sense of fear. I think I know what he really means.

"You mean steal some cattle?"

"Liberating them," he counters.

That vague tug of something forgotten happens again. I try to follow it, but my memory fails. There's something about cattle thieving and it's important but I can't bring it to mind no matter how I try. Which is strange because I've studied Scottish history most of my life, but it wasn't focused on the MacGregor clan. Maybe that's all it is.

"It's dangerous, though, right?"

"Aye."

"Don't do it," I say.

I hate the pleading note in my voice. The icy hand of dread reaches into my chest and grips my heart. Every beat pushes its chill out and through me. Something terrible is going to happen. I may not be able to pursue a romance with Duncan, but that sure doesn't mean I want something bad to happen to him.

"That's nae an option," he says.

"Why? You agree it's dangerous, so why do it? Don't."

A sense of urgency thrums in my head combining with that nagging knowing I've forgotten something. Something important. Like having left the oven on important.

What the devil is it?

"Lass, it's what we do," he says, laughing. "It's how we survive."

The storm of emotions is an assault inside my head. I know, with no reason or rhyme to it, that this is a moment. A moment on which everything hinges. If he goes, it will be bad. Epic bad.

"Duncan, please." I hate the note of begging in my voice. "This one time, don't go."

"Quinn." He says my name and it echoes in my head, reverberating around my skull as it contrasts with the memory of the dark stranger saying my name. "It's fine. I promise. Nothing will happen."

He stops, turning in and touches my face. He cups my chin in his hand and I'm staring into the icy blue of his piercing eyes.

"I like you. Please don't do this."

"I like you too," he says. "Quite a lot."

He's so close that the warmth of his breath passes across my face, and I flush hot. My skin tingles where he touches, and I want more. My lips tremble with desire to kiss him. I want to throw myself into his arms. I want to, but I can't.

He moves closer. The tiny distance separating us might as well be a gulf. I can't do this. As he leans in for a kiss, I jerk back.

"No," I say, shaking my head.

"Aye. All right."

He doesn't say more but I feel his hurt. He scratches his head and looks around before returning his gaze to mine. We stare at each other at an uncomfortable impasse. It continues until we're interrupted by the flutter of wings and we both look at the sound.

A raven caws as it passes over. Duncan makes the sign of the cross and mutters something under his breath. I watch the bird pass over and have to wonder if it really is following me.

"I need to get back," I say, pushing down my desire and the regret that blossoms as I say it.

"Are ya sure? You do nae have to."

His voice is a mix of sincerity and remorse. Every fiber of my being wants to say I'll stay. I want to spend time with him and explore these feelings. Maybe somehow understand this weird sense of knowing him better than I can possibly know anyone. Every fiber except the small voice of rationality. The voice of my heart that could never play someone, drag them along when I know there's no possibility of a future. That's not right and it's not me.

"Yeah," I say at last.

The word comes out in a huff, forced out as I make the only decision I can. I have to be true to myself. The crestfallen look on his face is as clear as a hurt puppy. As honest and blunt as he is in life, he'd be a terrible poker player. His emotions are all over his face. His handsome, strong jawed, wide-mouthed, hooked nose face.

God, I want to kiss him. To taste his lips. Touch that rough stubble on his cheeks. I want to but I won't. If this hurts him, imagine what it would be like for him when I return to my own time where I belong.

"All right," he says, not meeting my eyes.

He offers his hand and leads the way back to the village. We walk in a silence that is no longer comfortable. Though we're still holding hands, we're isolated in our own thoughts, wrapped in our pain. And pain it is. It hurts so much I want to cry but I can't let myself appear weak or irresolute.

An impossible situation. An impossible girl. What is this? Some Doctor Who episode?

When the village comes into sight, Duncan stops and lets go of my hand.

"I've got some work to tend to," he says. "Ya can make it the rest of the way?"

"Yeah," I say.

He opens his mouth as if he's going to say something but then he snaps it shut, turns, and strides off without a word. I stand on the path watching him leave and ring my hands in the cloth of my long skirt. The ache in my chest throbs in time with each beat of my heart. When he disappears around a corner, I force myself to turn and walk toward the village.

I hold myself together for at least four strides before the dam breaks. Tears stream down my face and the ache in my chest is so painful I'd fear it was a heart attack if I didn't know better. I stumble my way down the path to Alesoun's house, barely able to see past my bleary eyes.

"Witch!" a tiny voice yells as something pelts me in the arm.

"What?" I exclaim in pain and surprise, wiping at my eyes.

"Witch!" The one tiny voice is joined by a chorus of others.

Something hits me in the face with a splat. The smell of it turns my stomach. I raise my arms to protect my head. Something else hits me in the leg.

"Ow!"

Four young boys come up running circles around me. Something hits me in the back. Another of the boys throws a small rock that hits my arm. They are fast, staying out of reach as they chant and run their circle.

"Witch. Witch. Witch."

"Hey, stop," I yell.

Something else splats against my chest. I look down to see a nasty cow pie sliding down my chest. I break into a run, trying to get away, get to Alesoun, to shelter.

"Witch. Witch. Witch. Witch."

They give chase like a feral animal sensing fear and weakness. They pause only to grab small rocks and toss them before resuming the chase. I'm almost to the house when something hits me in the back of my head. I stumble forward and the world flashes to black.

"Aye!" an older, male voice yells.

"Back off now, ya hear?" Alesoun asks.

"I'll chap your hide, boys."

Duncan. It's Duncan who came to my most assuredly undeserved rescue.

Two sets of hands help me to my feet. I'm shaky on my feet but they steady me.

"Ach, are ya all right?" Alesoun asks.

"Fine," I say automatically. I touch the back of my head and feel a knot swelling there.

Tears break free, again as emotions—regret, anger, and depression—overwhelm me. I don't belong here. I have to get home.

"I'm sorry about that," Duncan says. "I'll be speaking to the boys' fathers."

I shake my head but that makes the pain worse. Alesoun and Duncan hover close, fussing, but I push them both away and try to stand on my own. A wave of dizziness passes over me and my knees buckle. They grab me but I push again, insisting to stand on my own.

"I'm fine," I say, looking at Duncan. "Aren't you supposed to be off stealing?"

The acid barb of my tone is biting. Duncan grimaces and his eyes narrow. He frowns as he takes a step back. I feel terrible for having done it, but it's the right thing to do.

"Aye," he says, a storm of emotions dancing unspoken across his face. "I'll be on my way then. Glad you're okay."

"Thanks," I say, affecting a coldness that I don't feel.

He stares for longer than I'm comfortable, but I meet his stare and wait. At last, he turns and walks away. My knees quiver and I almost fall, but Alesoun hooks her arm beneath mine to support me.

"Bit rough on the lad, weren't ya?" she asks.

"It's for the best," I mutter as we make our way into her house.

This witchcraft thing is getting worse. If the chief decides I'm a witch too, they'll banish me. Then I'll be well and truly screwed.

Chapter Sixteen

TODAY I'M ATTEMPTING to learn to weave a basket out of reeds. Alesoun and I moved a worktable out of her home to work in the sun. I stop once again to stare off at the horizon. The cold hard knot my guts have tied themselves into still hasn't let go. The men, including Duncan, have been gone for two days. I haven't slept more than a few minutes at a time since they left.

Every time I close my eyes, Duncan is there waiting, except he's badly hurt. Or he's dead, a zombie wandering through my dreams and taunting me. Asking me why. Why did you reject me? The same question I'm asking myself, even though I know the answer.

"Ach, quit your worrying, lass," Alesoun says, walking up behind me. "They'll be along soon enough."

"Yeah." I sigh, standing up and stretching.

"That is nae a basket," Alesoun says, giving my work a critical eye. "It will fall apart the moment ya put anything inside of it."

I stare at the almost shapeless bundle of heather roots and stalks that I've been attempting to weave together as she has tried to teach me. It's frustrating that she's right. There is no arguing about it. The basket should be at least mostly round, but my effort is more egg shaped with huge gaps.

I chew my lip and stare at the basket, trying to figure out what I did wrong. Suddenly the basket springs apart. One of the stalks whips painfully across my shin and I yelp as I jump away. Alesoun laughs. A deep, full laugh such as I've never heard from her before. Feeling sheepish I frown, my cheeks warming.

"I guess you're right," I say. "I'm no good at this."

"Aye! The look on your face..." Laughter fights for dominance over her words. "Ah, that was worth the time."

"Glad I can at least entertain you." I huff, taking my seat and picking up the fallen sticks that are supposed to be the framework of the basket.

Alesoun wipes tears from her eyes, still chuckling. A smile flits across my face. She's a good woman. Almost as outcast as I am here but with the disadvantage that this is her home. She doesn't have any hope of escaping back to her own time. Or some mysterious destiny to fulfill. This is the entirety of her life.

Shunned by her peers. Tolerated only for her skills in healing but even so looked on with derision and suspicion. Even now I feel the hateful glares cast at the two of us from the other women in the village. I get it, though. The idea of being banished from the village terrifies me.

The memory of my encounter with the Colquhouns is right there, ready to pounce. What if Duncan hadn't saved me? What would they have done? And if not them, then how would I get food? Shelter? Survival isn't easy.

"Weave them tighter," Alesoun says, coming over. She shows me how to do it, again.

I watch closely but despite the fact that it *looks* easy, hands-on practice has proven that it's far from it. All I can do is keep trying. She helps more, guiding my hands and correcting the work as I go. I lose track of time as we continue and soon enough there is at least the beginnings of a nice basket.

"Wow," I say, a sense of pride tingling as I look at my basket.

"Ach, nae too bad," Alesoun says. "You'll make a fine wife,

some day. Give yourself a few years at my knee and I'll teach ya the things you should already know."

Backhanded or not, I accept her compliment. She's the only person here who knows I'm not from this time, but she's right. If I grew up in this time, I'd probably know all these skills. I've seen little girls no more than five or six learning to do these chores in the village. I'd have been doing the same.

"What about you?" I ask, curiosity getting the best of me. We haven't talked much about her life here outside the obvious.

"What about me?"

"Don't you want a husband? Kids?"

Her face darkens but she doesn't look away.

"Tha was never going to be my life," she says, breaking eye contact and picking up the basket she is weaving.

It's clear she's done with the conversation but I'm not. I want to know. She's been so nice to me, and I don't understand the way they treat her.

"Why not?" I ask, almost pleading with her to trust me.

She stops bending the reed and stares at the partial basket. She hunches her shoulders as her cheeks flush. She shrugs and shakes her head before at last meeting my gaze.

"Because I'm touched. Like you." She makes the sign of the cross and her eyes dart up to heaven. "No matter how much a man might like the looks of ya, it do nae matter when it comes to matters of the soul."

"I don't get it. What does this, touch as you call it, have to do with anything? How is it a matter of the soul? You have skills in healing. That should be a good thing."

"Ach, lass. You know nothing."

The resounding truth in her words slices into my chest and twists painfully.

"You're right," I say, a massive weight dropping onto my shoulders.

It's soul crushing how little I know. I don't know how I got here or why I'm here. Don't know who the stranger on the moor was and how he seems to know me. I don't know how I'm going to get home. I don't even know why my stomach flutters and my heart palpitates every time Duncan looks at me. Is it love? Some biochemical reaction in the primal part of my brain deciding he's a good mate because of pheromones or his physicality.

"Ach, don't let it weight you." Alesoun places a friendly hand on my shoulder and pats my back. "You're young. You have a lot of life to live, to learn. You'll figure it out."

"Right." I shrug. "It doesn't feel like I will. What about you? Have you ever been in love?"

"Aye," she says, working her weaving.

"You have?" I ask. "Wow. Tell me, how do you know?"

A slow smile spreads over her face as she chuckles.

"You might as well ask how the sun rises in the morn. Or why the grass is green. Some things, lass, they just are. Love is, you know."

"That sounds nice and poetic, but it doesn't answer the question. How? How do you know it's love? Not—I don't know what you would call it—puppy love?"

"Ya feel it," she says. "In your heart, in your chest. In the way your guts twist up when you're with him and twist even more when you're nae."

"How do you know it's not just..." I trail off, unsure how to say what I'm thinking in a way that won't offend her. "How do you know it's not urges?"

Alesoun laughs, her full bellied almost guffaw. Tears fill her eyes because she's laughing so hard.

"Ya don't," she says. "But ain't nothing wrong with doing with your body what the Good Lord intended."

"Oh," I say, looking away but that only brings the gathering of village women and their glares into view.

One of them mouths 'witch' then makes the sign of the cross. Nausea clamps my stomach tight. I want to tell them off. I want to storm down there and yell, scream, and generally throw a fit but it won't do any good. If anything, it would only make things worse.

A scream in the distance stops any ideas of telling the women off. Alesoun and I leap to our feet, and the other women do the same. That scream sounded like a pained voice and as I look around to find a source. The sound repeats.

Alesoun and I pick up our skirts and run around the backside of her house. The sounds of rustling cloth and hard shoes follow us as the other women come behind us. A way off, dark shapes rush towards the village. What was fear dials up towards terror. Alesoun and I stop in our tracks, and I stare wide-eyed and open-mouthed, unable to speak or move.

"Are we under attack?" I ask, forcing the thought into words as numbness makes my limbs tingle.

"Are ya daft?" Agnes barks, appearing next to me and speaking with scorn and derision in her voice. "That's our men."

The terror in my heart doesn't diminish but instead switches purpose as deftly as a boxer weaving around his opponent's jabs. Our men and one of them is hurt. Badly, judging by the cries of pain. One thought pounds in my head and I give it voice.

"Duncan!"

I run. The men are distant shadows looming larger. Fear pulses in my veins, wicked cold, slicing through my heart. If he is hurt... or worse. The last words I had with him were harsh. He didn't deserve that and what if he—Another scream stops my runaway train of thought.

"Slow down, lass," Rob Macgregor says, grabbing me by my shoulders.

I struggle to get past him, but he tightens his grip and holds me in place.

"Let me go," I shout. "Who's hurt? Who is it?"

"Patrick," he says. "It's Patrick."

Patrick. Not Duncan. Guilt washes in behind the sense of

relief that it's not Duncan. But if it's Patrick and not Duncan, then where is Duncan?

I grab Rob in return.

"Where's Duncan?" I ask, my voice is a hoarse whisper. "Where is he?"

The dreams that have plagued me are right there, dancing behind my wide-open eyes. Duncan returning bloody and hurt. Dying or close enough.

"He's fine," Rob says.

"How bad is he? Is he hurt?"

"No, lass, I said he's fine. He's a way back, bringing the herd in," Rob says.

He's fine. He's fine. He's fine.

I repeat it over in my head. Breathe, Quinn, breathe. Furious with myself and this ridiculous display of emotion, I roughly grab a hold of myself, take a deep breath, and hold it. When I let it out slowly, I imagine calm and control spreading through my body. I repeat the breath again and do the same thing.

"Good, that's good," I say. The group of men carrying Patrick walk past on their way to the village. "I should help with Patrick."

"What do ya know of healing?" Rob asks.

"More than you'd think. I was training to be a—" I stop myself from saying *doctor*, knowing that would further mark me as an outlander witch. "A healer back home."

"Ah, no wonder you get along so well with Alesoun."

"Right," I say. "That's exactly it."

"Well, let's be about it then. If you'n know some healing arts, Patrick will need all you've got and I'm sure Alesoun will appreciate the help."

Together we run to catch up with the other men. They carry Patrick on their shoulders and straight inside Alesoun's home. Most of the men group outside the door, muttering and talking among themselves. All of them are stained with fresh blood. I'm not sure if anyone else is hurt or if the blood isn't theirs.

"Get some oil boiling," Chief Johnne MacGregor barks. "She'll be needing it."

Boiling oil? What are they planning to do?

I push past the gathered villagers, men and women, and force my way into Alesoun's home. Patrick is lying on the table, groaning. Blood covers his shirt, face, and arms, dripping onto the floor. Alesoun is leaning over, probing him with her fingers. He cries out in pain as she presses around his shoulder.

"God!" Patrick screams. "Can ya nae be a bit gentler?"

"Can ya nae learn to duck?" Alesoun asks. "You've a bullet in your shoulder. I need to know if you've broken the bone or not."

"If I 'ave?"

"You'll probably lose the arm."

"No," Patrick says, shaking his head. He tries to rise, but James and Johnne force him down onto the table and hold him there.

My stomach turns over and bile rises in my throat. Amputating an arm, no antiseptic, no anesthesia. I can't imagine anything worse.

"Lie still, lad," Johnne orders. "She'll fix ya right up. Now come on, don't be weak."

"Let me see," I say, my former, if incomplete, training as a doctor kicking in.

I may not have finished a degree, but I am sure I know more than Alesoun about the structure of the human body and how to treat wounds. James and Johnne look askance to Alesoun before letting me in.

"Have a look while I get the oil," Alesoun says, moving aside.

Patrick grimaces as I step into his field of view. "Ach, don't need a pretty lass to be seeing me all banged up like this."

"You're fine," I say, inspecting the hole in his shoulder.

It's jagged and rough. Gently, I run my hands over his shoulder and feel behind, looking for an exit wound.

"Well, you're a might gentler than Alesoun," he says. "I'd right enjoy your touch in friendlier—agh!"

I push my finger into the wound when I don't find an exit. The tip of my finger touches cold steel. Exactly what I feared. The bullet is lodged deep in his shoulder, close to the bone.

"Good news is I don't think you've broken any bones," I say.

"Ach, that does sound right good, doesn't it?"

"Bad news is, that bullet has to come out. Do any of you have whiskey?"

"Here," James says, pulling out a flask.

I take it, uncap it, then pour it into Patrick's open mouth. He sputters then swallows.

"Gah, you're trying to drown me?"

"You're going to want it," I say, then pour some over his wound.

He screams in surprised pain. I finish off the last swallow myself to steel my nerves. It burns its way down my esophagus and ignites a boiling fire in my stomach.

"Make way," Alesoun says behind me.

The house always smells, which I've gotten used to, but the scent of blood, piss, and now Alesoun walking in with boiling oil is enough to make my stomach revolt. She has rags wrapped around the handle of a metal pan filled with oil. The oil bubbles and pops. I don't know what she's going to do with that, but I don't think it's going to be good.

"We have to take the bullet out before you do anything else," I say.

"And how will you do that, lass? It's lodged deep."

"If we don't, he'll not have use of his arm. That's the best case. Worst case the wound will infect and kill him."

"Aye," Alesoun agrees, "but that doesn't answer the question, now does it?"

I frown. She's right. I don't have any surgical tools or an easy way to dig a bullet out.

"I can do it," I say firmly. "But I'm warning you, Patrick, this is going to hurt."

"Will I be able to keep and use my arm?" he asks through gritted teeth.

"It's your best chance," I say. "But I can't promise it."

He looks at Alesoun. James and Johnne look at her too, trusting her opinion.

"She's not wrong," Alesoun says. "I do nae have tha skill to remove tha bullet though."

"Fine," Patrick sobs. "Do it."

"Give me your knife," I say, holding out my hand towards the two men.

James hands me his knife. I hold it in my hand for a moment, feeling its weight and balance. It's a good knife. I place the tip above the open wound, take a deep breath, and slice down. Patrick cries out and bucks, fighting to get away.

"Hold him!" I yell.

James and Johnne grab him.

"Get in here and help," Johnne orders and two more men join the struggle to hold Patrick down.

I place the knife parallel to his collar bone beside the bullet hole. Another deep breath to steady my hands, and then I push in and slice across. He fights but the men hold him. The screaming, even the staring onlookers, are all part of another universe. For me the entirety of my attention is on getting this bullet out.

Having widened the opening, I use the tip of the knife to probe until I feel it hit the steel of the bullet. Carefully, I work it out, a centimeter at a time. I don't know how long it takes but it feels like an eternity before there is the gleam of the steel and am able to grab it out with my fingers.

"Got it!" I exclaim, holding it up proudly.

A few cheers echo through the house. Not resounding but at least some positive response. Patrick is bleeding profusely but there's no spurting so by some miracle the bullet and my makeshift surgery missed any arteries. His color is fading though, and his eyes are drifting shut. He's losing too much blood.

"I need a needle and thread," I order.

"I've got oil here, ready," Alesoun says. "You can cauterize the wound with it."

"No," I say. "Needle and thread. Let me finish this."

Alesoun stares at me with not only a lack of comprehension but disbelief.

"Alesoun, please."

She shakes her head and goes to her small cabinet, then returns with a needle and thread. I set to work sewing him up neatly. At last, I straighten. The stiffness in my back from being hunched over him this entire time is accented by my spine cracking.

"There," I say. "He needs rest, but he should be okay."

"Good," Johnne says.

I'm suddenly and acutely aware of the stares. It feels as if I'm on display or I walked into class and forgot to dress for the day. I turn around to face the crowd. Dozens of eyes are all trying to see into the house and witness what the outlander is doing to Patrick.

I lock eyes with Agnes who is closest to the door. She has a dark, almost evil look on her face. Her lips are pressed tight, and she narrows her eyes. We lock gazes for a heartbeat, then she shakes her head ever so slightly. Deliberately slow, she makes the sign of the cross and turns her back.

James and Johnne lift Patrick and carry him out of the house. My stomach sinks to the floor, then a wave of nausea so strong I almost lose it strikes. I wrap my arms around myself and rub my arms, breathing through the nausea.

I may have saved Patrick's life, but I have done nothing to improve my standing with the rest of the villagers who seem more convinced than ever that I am a witch.

Chapter Seventeen

THE VILLAGE IS BRIGHTLY LIT by the central fire. It's built bigger than it has been since I've been here and the carcass of one of the cows they've stolen roasts on a spit over it. The rich scent of the meat fills the air as its juices sizzle in the fire, mixing with the music of bagpipes, flutes, and drums.

Villagers dance around the roasting meat, boys and girls swinging each other with such wild abandon that more than once I'm sure one or the other is going to land in the bonfire. Thankfully, by some miracle, no one has, yet.

Everyone is gathered which includes Alesoun and me. We are surrounded by the clan, yet they still manage to make me feel their distance. It's obvious in their sharp glances, quick signs of the cross, or warding against the evil eye. I'm an outcast. I don't belong here, and they want to make sure I know it.

It doesn't stop the fun though. Even for me. Though at moments it feels like it, not all the villagers are mean. A long table is set up and laden with food: breads, cheeses, nuts, fruits, smoked fish, and even some sweets. There is plenty of drink to be had and I've had more than one mug of the sharp and bitter ale. After the third one, it doesn't taste so bad.

"He's making eyes at ya," Alesoun says, drunkenly grabbing my arm.

She speaks in a stage whisper, loud enough that the closest people turn and look. She has a big smile on her face as she weaves on her feet. I glance in the direction she's looking then turn quickly away when I see Duncan staring. He's standing with Robert and some other men, talking and drinking.

"I see that," I say.

My head is light and the world around me has a slight rocking as if someone broke the equilibrium of the ground. Or the earth is a ship, racing through the waves of space, and the ground is rising and falling as we crest each one.

I can't keep myself from smiling. The firelight casts an intriguing orange glow on his face that highlights his strong jaw. I like the way his eyes glitter with the reflected light. It's as if they're burning themselves. Burning because of me, at least in my slightly tipsy imagination. Warmth flashes across my skin, but it's probably because I'm too close to the fire. That must be it.

The music is loud as if it is at war with the conversations and laughter. Alesoun laughs loudly, squeezes my arm, then wanders off, leaving me on my own. I glance in Duncan's direction again. He's still staring.

Oddly uncomfortable, I walk around the outskirts of the gathering and bask in the happiness of the people. Their joy is a palpable warmth beyond that the fire casts. Their lives are hard. Every day is a struggle for survival, but they are happier and more alive than anyone I've ever known. More than I've ever been.

It touches something deep inside. That sense of déjà vu pulls at the fog of forgotten memories. A mix of feeling as if I've been here before, experienced this, and knowing that there is something important I've forgotten. It's frustrating to not be able to recall it. Like having something stuck in your teeth that no matter how you try you can't get it to work free.

All my life I've felt I didn't belong, not quite fitting in no matter where I was. Growing up I blamed losing Mom young as I did. Her loss was so sudden and unexpected, it taught me to not trust anything. Nothing is forever, even the one constant you should be able to rely on.

I push aside those worries and let myself bask in the moment. The joy the Clan takes in the moment is an energy that I can't help but let affect me. It lifts the dark cloud of my thoughts. An effusive feeling of warmth and love fills my heart and then I realize a truth.

I'm happy. Here.

Relaxation comes with understanding. These people, even Agnes and her group, they're good people. Living each moment to the fullest. The men have been nothing but kind and honorable. Alesoun is, well she's the mother I missed out on growing up. I love these people and for the first time in my life, I don't feel completely out of place.

An older man with a long, thick rust colored beard steps out into the center of the crowd to stand close to the fire. The bonfire outlines him so that he looks almost like a phoenix in human form, as if he's rising from the flames. He raises his arms, and the crowd falls silent. The music changes from a raucous Highland explosion, dropping down until there is only a soft, repeating beat on the drums.

"Come now, listen and I'll tell ya the tale of Crann Bethadth, the Tree of Life itself," he says. He's a skilled showman. The lilt of his voice, the motions he makes, and the way the crowd responds; they're enthralled and so am I. "Now you'll well know that Crann Behadth is considered to be Irish in origin, but tonight I'm going to give you deeper truths.

"Our cousins on the Island do nae even know this. The Tree is much older by far. Did the Vikings not have their Yggradasil? Even the ancient Egyptians knew of the Tree of Life and does nae the Good Book itself tell the tale of Adam and Eve? And what cause their fall from tha Lord's perfect garden?"

"The tree," a young boy exclaims.

"Aye, you're a well-schooled lad, blessings on your mother. A tree. *The* tree. The Tree of Life, no matter what name you give it. But this is a tale of Scotland. A tale of our ancestors and what tale would be complete without the entrance of the Fair folks?"

The crowd makes appreciative sounds of *oohs* and *ahs*, and I join along with them, swept away by his storytelling. His voice is rich and entrancing. The beating of the drums perfectly accent his words. I move closer and no one gives me a second look. At least in this moment, I feel welcome.

"You'll know the Fair ones, the ones who came before," he continues. "Who we know but rarely encounter and when we do, you do nae know if it will be a good or a bad event in your life, but an event it will be. The Fair ones are connected to the tree itself, you see.

"Tha Queen of the Fair, Queen Maebe herself, was bathing in a pool when a poor lost shepherd came upon her, seeking a lost lamb. When he stepped around the tree, he knew he was seeing tha which he never should. The Queen of the Fair in all her glory, bathed only in water and moonlight. Even so, he felt what any man would feel seeing such a sight, despite his fear."

My breath catches in my chest as the image is drawn in my mind's eye by his words. I'd swear no one else is breathing either. I risk a glance. The crowd's eyes glisten and like me, everyone is seeing the pictures he's painting with his words. The only person who doesn't seem to be enraptured is Duncan. He sees my glance and my heart leaps into my throat. My stomach clamps and a shiver starts under my ribs, working its way up.

"Tha poor shepherd, he stared, stopped in his tracks by the beauty he saw and the desire it stirred in him. As he stood enraptured, two of the Fair folk appeared and took him into custody. For the Fair Queen was no sight for mortal eyes. They dragged him before their Queen and forced him to his knees.

"And she looked on him with the disdain of the Fair. He trembled and begged her forgiveness and I know he'd not be ashamed to say he groveled. What man would nae when faced down by the Queen herself?

"His pleas were as naught to the Queen. She passed her judgment, telling him he would come with them to the Bright Lands. Well, as ya know, in the Bright Lands time does run differently, but by her decree he was to spend one week in her palace. And if after a week he had not partaken of any of the delights, if he was able to hold strong to his will, she would return him to this world.

"And though he was filled with terror such as to almost kill the desire her pure form created, he understood this was to be his test. So it was he agreed he would go with her. He knew he could nae fight and win against the lads that held him and this was his one chance to return to his home."

Desire burns in my lower belly, either from the tale, or perhaps from my inebriation. Biting my lower lip, I glance at Duncan. He's still staring at me and now his face is naked with desire, much as the man in the tale.

I feel it too. Of course I want him. He's an incredibly handsome man but it's not only his looks. This doesn't feel like simple lust, no matter how much I wonder what his lips would taste like. It's this feeling, this understanding that I know him. Know him in a way that our short time together can never explain. In a way I've never known or felt about anyone before in my life.

"And on the seventh day of his captivity," the storyteller continues, and I realize I've missed part of the story while lost in Duncan's gaze, "he went again to the tree that grew in the middle of her palace. The silvery light it gave off called to him. There was a piece of fruit hanging this day from a low branch. Rich, vibrant, tempting his great hunger for it had been more than seven days since he had taken food.

"With a trembling hand, he reached for the fruit but as his fingers were about to close upon its ripe richness, he noticed a thing about the tree itself. The branch from which the fruit hung had a dark mar upon it. Such was this mar on what was otherwise a most perfect tree, that it pulled his attention away from his great hunger.

"Instead of grabbing the fruit, he put his hand on the scar and it was as if a veil was lifted from his eyes. When he did, the great beauty and shining perfection of the palace faded, for you see he saw it as it really was. The glamour of the Queen was removed.

"'Now you see our truth,' the Queen said from behind him. And when he turned, she was no longer a beautiful woman to be desired but a hag, bent and lined with age. 'Do you still desire me? Will you take me as a man takes a woman?' Our poor shepherd shook his head, denying the Queen though he was fearful that in rejecting her he might lose his life.

"The Queen didn't harm him, though. Instead, she nods and smiles, a toothless smile. She tells him when he returns to his world to remember the Fair Folk but more than that to dream. She touched his forehead and bright lights exploded in his head and he remembered the dreams he had as a young lad. Dreams of owning his own land, of living free, of having a beautiful family of his own.

"When his head cleared, he was home, as you well know, and the lost lamb was at his feet. He knew that he'd been given a gift. That the gift of the Tree was to dream. And that, dear friends, is the greatest gift that the Fair folk can impart."

The crowd explodes, clapping with a furiousness as the tale comes to an end. The music resumes and everyone leaps to their feet dancing. Duncan makes his way through, weaving around the dancers with the skill of a man used to the field of battle. When he stands before me, his musky scent fills my senses.

"Might I have this dance?" he asks, holding out his hand.

There's a fluttering sensation in my chest and tears well in my eyes. Biting my lip, I nod as I take his hand. His smile breaks across his face like the sun bursting past the horizon. The tune is a lively, quick beat. I've never been much of a dancer, much less knowing the style of dance being done here, but I let him take the lead.

As we step onto the open ground and join the others, it feels natural. Right. As if this really isn't something new at all. He puts one arm behind his back, keeping my hand in his other. He rises onto the balls of his feet, and I mimic his motion. He bounces and kicks a foot out in time with the music. I stumble trying to imitate him and he laughs.

"Nae, m'lady, like this," he says, holding me up by my arm.

He repeats the step. This time he moves slowly through the actions. The booze has definitely gone to my head. I giggle, and my head is light and my heart palpitating.

"Are you insulting the quality of my dance, sir?"

"No, m'lady," he says smiling. "It's quite fine... if'n you were a goat."

"Ach," I gasp, mimicking the sound Alesoun makes to me so often. "I cannot believe such an insult to my honor."

I throw my free hand up to my forehead and look skyward as if I'm endlessly offended.

"M'lady, I will nae allow anyone to ever besmirch your honor."

The laughter is gone from his voice. I look at him quickly. The earnest seriousness on his face makes my breath catch in my chest. His beautiful yet icy eyes bore into mine with so much intensity my throat is dry. My lip trembles as I become acutely aware of the burning warmth of his hand holding mine. Wordlessly, I move towards him, my lips closing with his.

"Chief Johnne!"

The voice yelling for the chief breaks the moment as the music, clapping, and singing screeches to a halt. A young boy, probably in his teens, stumbles into the open space in front of the fire. He comes to a stop, resting his hands on his knees while panting heavily. When he looks up, his eyes are wide and his face smeared with dirt. There's a trail of blood running down the side of his face from a nasty cut on his forehead.

"What is it, William?" Chief Johnne asks, emerging from the crowd and towering over the boy.

"The king," William gasps. He digs into his pouch and pulls out a crumpled, dirty piece of paper. "Colquhouns are to arm themselves. Against us."

Chapter Eighteen

TENSION CRASHES over the village as if it was carpet bombed. A silence so deep that I don't even hear the insects holds everyone.

Chief Johnne grabs the paper and turns so that the light of the fire illuminates it for him to read. His face becomes stonier as he reads, his lips pulling down into a frown as his brow furrows. . His eyes go over the lines and I wait, like everyone, with bated breath.

"It's true," he says at last. "The English King James has authorized the Colquhouns to arm themselves against the scourge of the MacGregors. Our deeds at Glen Fruin were 'without pity or compassion'. Our 'wicked and unhappy' race is to be 'exterminated and rutted out.'"

An eruption of arguments explodes as everyone shouts and yells in their own defense. A raven's caw echoes in my head. Numbly, I drop Duncan's hand. That memory I couldn't quite recall crashes into my head with all the force of a speeding semi-truck. It bursts through the barriers of forgetting and slams into my metaphorical face.

MacGregor. The MacGregors go on a cattle raid, but the Colquhouns use it to persuade the King of England to basically deputize them. That was the raid they just did. The writ is only the beginning. It's going to get so much worse. They won the battle, but they lost the war without even knowing it.

Their rivals, the Colquhouns, and behind them the Campbells, are luring them into a trap. Those two clans are already maneuvering against them politically and have primed the King of England to give them the writ.

This declaration is only the start. The clan will unite and go to fight and when they win that battle, the final piece is in place. After they win, it will become illegal to be a MacGregor. This entire village, all these people I've only just come to know, will become outlaws. Even the women and children.

The MacGregors will be hunted mercilessly. There are horrible accounts of turning in the heads of MacGregors as payment for crimes. Of wholesale slaughter of the MacGregor clan. There were no complete records of how many MacGregors were killed but every man, woman, and child is in mortal danger.

Cold sweat trickles down my spine as the world spins. I ride waves of nausea that crash into me and stumble away from the crowd. How do I stop this? Is this why I'm here? What if Alesoun is killed? Duncan?

Moving away from the group, I retreat, needing to be alone. Even though the women have been less than welcoming, I don't want to see any of them dead.

The raven's caw echoes in my ears. As I run away, it continues cawing until I realize it's not only in my head. The big black bird is sitting on the edge of Alesoun's roof, staring with its glistening black eyes. In its raucous caw, I hear words: *I warned you. I am the harbinger of death. Find your destiny.*

I'm scared. Terrified. I don't know what to do. Don't know how or why I'm here. Despite the open air and space, I'm claustrophobic. The air itself is crushing me. I have to get away.

I burst into a run, going past the houses and out onto the open grass of the highlands. The scent of the early heather in the air helps soothe my nerves. The silvery moon hangs half full, looking and feeling so close as if I should be able to reach out and touch it.

They're going to die.

I don't know who or how many, but some if not all of them are going to die. And I can't stop it. I drop to my knees, overcome by the weight crushing down. I sob, unable to contain the storm of sadness.

"Quinn!" Duncan calls.

Damn it, I don't want him to see me like this. I rub my face, furiously trying to dry my tears that won't stop. I take a deep breath, trying to find some sense of composure. Damn it, I'm too drunk. This isn't the time to be dealing with this or him.

"Here," I say when I feel a little less overwhelmed. I stand up and turn towards his voice.

"Ach, there ya are. Ya ran off. I was worried. Are you okay?" He walks closer, staring at my face. "Have ya been crying?"

I want to be brave, to deny that I have, but my tongue won't form the lie. Besides, what is there that's brave about not admitting I cry? Am I some emotional shut off?

"Yeah," I say, wiping the last of my tears.

"Why? What's the matter?"

I shake my head, biting my lip to keep myself from breaking down into tears again.

"It's nae the King's writ, is it? What do we care for his proclamations? We're Scotsman. I will nae take a knee to some English King."

He takes my hands into his and squeezes them, attempting to be reassuring.

"Duncan," I say, touching his face. His rough stubble pokes at my fingertips as I trail along his cheek. "You sweet, brave man."

"You think I'm brave?" he asks, a boyish grin on his face, and he moves in closer.

My heart races, and all the fear and worry is thrust aside by the rush of blood to my head and lower bits. A burning inferno of sudden and surprising desire. He's so close, dominating the space.

"I do," I say breathlessly.

"You're beautiful," he whispers, leaning in.

"Thank you. I—"

His lips on mine cut off my words.

His kiss is the best kiss I've ever had. His lips are soft yet insistent. Sweet but with hints of the bitter ale we've both been drinking. I close my eyes as we kiss but the myriad of stars I was staring up into remain in my head, spinning as he wraps his arms around me and pulls me close.

He breaks the kiss at last but keeps his hold around me. My breasts are crushed against his chest so tight I can feel his heart thrumming. We're both breathing heavily, staring into each other's eyes.

"I've wanted to do that since I first laid eyes on you," he says.

I can't help but smile as my lips tingle. I want to kiss him again. I could kiss him forever. One long, unending kiss that continues until the stars fall from the sky.

But even drunk, reality pushes in and with reality comes fear. I know how bad this is going to get. I've spent most of my life studying Scotland and now that I remember what happens to the MacGregor Clan, I can't ignore it. The dark times coming for Clan MacGregor are going to be so much worse than he can possibly understand.

"Duncan, what are you going to do?"

His eyes twinkle with starlight and his grin turns mischievous.

"Nothing more than you willingly invite."

I shake my head and push him back to stand on my own. I cross my arms over my chest.

"No, Duncan. Not that. Not now. About the King's writ."

"Bah, we'll fight," he says, making a dismissive gesture.

"You can't," I say.

"Ach, I can. We can. We'll win too. God hisself is on the sides of the MacGregors. Those Colquhouns won't know what hit them."

"No," I say, raising my voice. Fear makes my tone sharper than I want but I can't help it. "You can't. I mean it. Trust me, Duncan. You can't win. It won't go the way you expect. It will be bad."

"What are you on about, lass?" he asks, shaking his head.

"Don't fight them," I say. "Please."

God, he has to listen to me. How do I get him to understand? I know what's coming and I can't spell it out because he'd never believe it.

"You've nothing to worry about," Duncan says with confident swagger. "We'll win and I'll be fine. Do nae doubt my skill with a sword."

I shake my head violently, trying to clear the alcohol and fear so I can come up with a rational argument he'll listen to. "It's not that. It's that you will win. I'm telling you, it will not come out the way you expect. It will be so much worse."

"What are you trying to say? What, can you tell the future?"

"You have to trust me," I plead. "Please."

"Ach," Duncan says, throwing his hands up and stepping back. Then he breaks my heart when he makes the sign of the cross. "You can't know the future and if'n you do, then maybe I should have listened to Agnes."

He turns his back and strides away to the village. As a raven cries, despair deeper than anything I've ever experienced washes over. These people who've taken me in, who've cared for me, and this man I have feelings for is going to die. And there's nothing I can do about it.

Chapter Nineteen

THE MID-MORNING SUN streams over the assembled villagers. The youngest children clutch at their mothers' skirts while the older ones cheer and jeer with the adults. Chief Johnne stands tall, surrounded by the group, huge arms crossed over his chest, silently listening as the men of the village voice their thoughts.

"We cannae stand by and let them arm against us," Patrick yells, and the voices of the crowd rise in assent.

I sit in the shadows of one of the houses, working the butter churn for Alesoun. I'm not part of the village and I can't face their looks. I especially can't face Duncan, not after last night, but I have to see how this plays out.

Maybe inspiration will come, and I'll see a way to stop this. Get them to... what? Not join the rest of their clan? It won't stop the King's next action. I have no idea how to stop this now that it's in motion. If they don't go and fight, the rest of the clan will still go and it's the next battle that pushes it all over the edge.

"He's nae my king!"

"What right does he have? Ordering them to arm against us?"

"Listen," Duncan says, stepping over to stand next to Chief

Johnne who has remained silent so far. "Of course we are nae going to stand by and let them attack us. But we cannae fight their entire clan alone."

"What are we going to do?"

I watch the folks of the village argue while slowly working the butter churn. The sound of the milk splashing inside of it mimics the way my stomach feels, filled with churning acid. They've been debating and arguing since the sun rose.

Duncan hasn't looked in my direction. Not once. Not so much as a glance.

Rationally, I know it's for the best. Tomorrow night, I'm supposed to meet the stranger by the standing stone. While I've debated whether or not I will go, it now feels like the right decision. I clearly don't belong here. This is about to go from bad to worse and somehow, I need to get back to my own time.

But it hurts. It hurts so damn much. What sense does that make? If this is really the right move, the right thing to do, can't it at least hurt less? It feels like something is tearing inside my chest, sharp claws ripping my heart all while the villagers continue to debate and argue. As I watch I can't help but imagine what might happen to each of them. Those dark thoughts hurt more than I can stand.

"All right," Chief Johnne says, speaking at last. "Listen. I do nae doubt that Alisdair will call a gathering. Until we know what he is planning, all else is speculation."

The crowd rumbles but no one disagrees.

He straightens to his full height, looking over the people of his village. "Now we 'ave work to be done. Get yourselves to it."

"Aye, that's the right move, Johnne," Alesoun says from behind me, and I jump.

"Oh, I didn't hear you," I say, heart thumping.

"You're nae here at all, how can ya?"

Warmth flushes my cheeks at her soft reprimand.

"Here, give me the churn. Can I trust ya to come back with some berries this time if I send ya out?"

"Of course," I say, standing up and stretching the stiff muscles of my back.

"Of course, she says." Alesoun tsks. "I sent ya out before and did I get any berries? Do nae let yourself be distracted, lass. Get me the berries and get back. All this excitement, we need be preparing. There will be a gathering and that is no small thing to cook for. I'll need do my part for the clan."

"What is a gathering?"

Alesoun sighs and shakes her head.

"Ach, lass, ya know nothing. A gathering is when the clan chief calls the clan together to discuss clan business."

"But I thought Johnne was the chief?"

"Aye, he is, of the village. He's nae chief of the whole clan though. He cannae handle a proclamation from the King of England."

Knowledge burns on the tip of my tongue. I clench my teeth to hold it back. Even though she knows my secret, I can't tell her. It's too much and here, at this time, what is she going to do to change their fate? All I would be doing is giving her the same burden I'm carrying. If anyone can do anything to stop it, it's going to be one of the men. I'm a really long time before any kind of women's liberation.

"Oh. What do you think they will do then?" I ask, knowing the answer, but hoping by some miracle I'm wrong. Maybe I'm remembering my history wrong. Maybe the texts I read were wrong. Something. Anything.

"If'n I know Chief Alisdair at all, it will be settled with swords before words. Ach, men folks." She shakes her head while making a disapproving sound. "Always thinking with their cocks and steel, nae with their words and their brains."

That makes me smile. "I get that. It doesn't really change."

131

"There you go, taking away any hint of hope I might have had," she says.

"Sorry," I say, ducking my head in a sort of apology. "Alesoun?" Her mouth twists with aggravation but she arches an eyebrow. "The tale at the fire was that true?"

"True as tales ever are," she says with a shrug then resumes churning.

"I've heard that before, about the Fae and their food."

"Aye. Time is different for the Fair folks and if'n ya eat the food of the fae, you're bound to them, same as blood." I chew my lower lip unsure why that part of the tale stuck with me. "Right, now off with ya," Alesoun says, shooing me away. "Do nae come back with less than a full basket. Ya hear?"

I nod as I pick up the basket from the shelf next to the door and head for the hills. Filling the basket is not going to be an easy task. It's a big basket for one but it's also not as if the berries grow thickly anywhere that I've seen.

As I make my way past the herd of grazing cows, their earthy scent is an assault on my senses. One of them stops grazing and turns its large head to watch me pass. It's thick and rust colored. Its shaggy hair shimmies as it snorts and shivers. I strain my neck to watch it over my shoulder as I move past it. I have that strange feeling I'm being watched, but I don't see anything besides the one cow out of the entire herd.

Quinn.

Someone whispers my name. Chills raise the hairs on the back of my neck and I shiver, looking quickly around for the source. I don't see anyone. There's no one for as far as I can see. I'm alone, striding across the open fields of the highlands.

It must be my imagination. My nerves are shot. Knowing what is coming has put me on edge. I pointedly ignore what happened with Duncan. Which has nothing to do with anything. Nope. Not a thing.

Suspicious, though, of everything, I keep one eye on the cow until I move around a ridge and lose sight of it.

To my right a bird caws. I whip my head in that direction in time to see a black shape dropping out of the sky. It comes to a landing on a rock outcropping. It's a raven. Again. Great. I pause and stare, but Alesoun's voice in my head pushes me forward. The raven watches as I come closer, occasionally hopping from foot to foot. When I'm an easy stone's throw away from it, I stop and stare at the stupid black bird.

"What?" I ask. "What do you want? Why do you keep following me?"

It tilts its shiny black head to one side as if asking in return what I'm doing.

"I'm sick of you. Sick of all this. I want to go home."

I spot a nice size rock close to my feet. I bend down and grab the rock. It fits nicely into my hand. I haul back and throw the rock at the raven. Unsurprisingly, I miss it. The rock bounces off the stone a foot to the raven's left and ricochets into the rolling grass. The raven doesn't even bother to fly off. Instead, it spreads its wings, caws, then closes its wings and resumes staring with glassy black eyes filled with reproach. Hitching the basket higher on my arm, I meet the raven's dark glare with one of my own then march past, pointedly ignoring the damn bird.

Tomorrow, I'll meet the stranger and find out how to get home. All I have to do is survive until then. Survive and not screw anything up. Like I have with Duncan.

Regret rises in my throat with an acidic burn. I like him. How is this fair? I can't fall for him. I can't explore these feelings he evokes because I don't belong here. Stupid songs. Stupid poets. Stupid heart. What is this I feel for him if not love? The way it feels like I've known him so much longer than I have. The way he makes my heart speed up. Makes me feel bigger, better for being around him.

It can't be desire only. I'm not even considering how he looks, which is great, thank you very much. Those bulging arms, the strong jaw, and those eyes! My god, he could probably charm the pants off any girl he wants with his eyes alone. I want him. He 'turns me on' or whatever but that's far from all I want.

I want to know him. Know him for real. The way it feels I know him, as if I know everything about him. I want to know his wants, needs, and desires. Know what his dreams are and his nightmares too. I want him to know me too.

This isn't simple young lust. It can't be. I've never been in love but I've sure as hell dreamed about it all my life. It's the one thing I've wanted that my life to date has made me think I'd never find. Someone who wants me for me.

Most guys want 'social media' perfection. The perfect wife, with the perfect body, all shown with perfect lighting, camera angles, and make up exactly done. They don't want the real girl. The one who looks like shit in the morning. The one who doesn't bother getting out of her sweats and tee on a lazy day. The one who didn't do last night's dishes because she was busy binge watching the newest season of her favorite show on streaming.

They don't want the reality; they want the fiction. Our entire society, the one I'm from anyway, is built around false pretenses. We sell our dreams to each other on social media.

None of that is true with Duncan. There's no other me for him to see than the me that is here. No makeup, no cameras, no perfect lighting but he keeps coming back. Even after I've been such an utter bitch to him. And the worst part of it all is I still think I'm right. I can't get involved with him.

This current upset they're all dealing with; I know where it's going to go. It's going to mean war. Historically, these events lead up to the literal outlawing of the MacGregor name. I knew I'd forgotten something but how I forgot that detail of history is unbelievable. If my memory is right, they'll attack the Colquhouns and win despite the odds being against them. And that is all it will take. They win and after that, King James outlaws the name.

The MacGregors will be hunted. Forced to change their names and hide. A lot of them will retreat further into the Highlands, where they will earn their nickname, Children of the Mist. The Campbells and the Colquhouns will put bounties on their heads and the crimes that will be committed against them are atrocities.

How do I stop that? Should I stop it?

It's so much different than studying words in a history book when you are here. When you meet and get to know the people. They're not words on paper; they're living, breathing souls. People with hopes, dreams, and personalities.

I don't even want Agnes, as mean as she has been to me, to suffer what I know is coming. I have no idea how many, if any, of the MacGregors in this village will be killed but the odds are great that it will be a lot, if not most, of them.

My thoughts run away as I gather berries as I find them. The basket is about a quarter full, nowhere near what Alesoun asked me to get, so I keep on walking and looking for more bushes. When my belly rumbles, I realize I didn't pack any food. Shrugging, I snitch a few of the berries to take the edge off as I walk and pick.

At least I don't see the stupid bird any longer, which is fine by me. I'm not really comfortable having a black, feathered stalker while I do my work. I've not been much help to Alesoun. The only thing I've shown any talent for is churning butter, but I want to get a full basket of berries. Alesoun has been very kind, putting me up and teaching me how to survive. The least I can do is get the berries right.

As I stride along, passing standing stones surrounded by purple heather, I come to a peat bog. The ground is soft and mucky, and it forces me to pick my way carefully through it. I focus on one foot in front of the other until there is the splashing of falling water on the air. The sound of the running water makes me realize how incredibly thirsty I am. I emerge from the boggy land and see something sparkling a dozen yards ahead that must be a stream. I head towards it.

The creek tumbles down the highlands, falling off a rock outcropping, causing the sound from the tiny waterfall. I climb a small hill to see the water running below me.

A woman dressed all in white, is kneeling next to the water. She's doing something; I can't make out what, but the water downstream from her runs as red as blood.

Chapter Twenty

IS SHE DYEING CLOTH? *In the river? Do they even have red dye?*

"Hello," I say when I get within hailing distance.

The woman doesn't look up or stop her work. Maybe she didn't hear me. I walk closer, really wanting a drink, but not of dye filled water. My dry throat aches with the idea of its offered relief. The woman continues working the cloth, plunging it in and out of the stream. I don't see her doing anything with any kind of dye, but the closer I get the deeper the red of the water.

I don't want to startle the woman, so I angle myself to reach the water a few yards downstream from her. Perhaps she is hard of hearing and the last thing I want is to surprise her. That could be dangerous. When I reach the stream, I get a good view of her work. She is washing clothes in the water. She dunks them in and out of the stream then slaps the cloth down on a rock. After that, she lifts the cloth and twists. Bright red water streams out of the cloth, joining the stream and causing the color.

"Hello," I say again.

The woman doesn't look over, so I walk closer. A tangy, almost coppery scent fills the air. Something about the odor hints of something wrong, something foul.

"Excuse me, I don't want to startle you."

I motion with my hand, trying to catch her attention. I'm only a few feet away when she stops. She stares at the cloth in her hand with her shoulders hunched. She turns slowly towards me and fear flutters in my chest.

Her matted gray hair is thick and knotted, hanging in such a way as to hide her face as she moves. When I see her face, she's old. Ancient would be more accurate, lines so deep on her face they could be valleys of their own. Her eyes are milky white as if covered with cataracts. She smiles, a joyless, toothless grin that stops me in my tracks. In her hand the cloth drips red and I realize, knowing it straight into my core, that it isn't dye dripping off the cloth. It's blood.

My eyes dart to the cloth, only for a second, but when I return them to the woman she's gone. Goose pimples race along my arms and chills go down my spine. I want to run but I'm frozen in place, staring at the empty space where a moment before the woman was.

A raven caws and the paralysis breaks. I do the only sensible thing I can think of: I run.

I run across the green grass of the highlands, through the azure blue sky, heart pounding in my ears as my breath comes shorter and shorter. A stitch forms in my side and some unknowable distance behind me I hear laughter.

I stumble more than once, landing hard and scraping my knees and hands. I barely notice the pain because adrenaline is still pumping through me. I'm so scared, I leap up each time and continue running. I run until I see the village. I pause to catch my breath, but the back of my neck tingles and that sense of danger is too much.

I resume my run, barreling past the cows and almost tripping over a goat. I stumble into the open ground at the center of the village. The group of women that work in front of Agnes' house stop to stare. I can't catch my breath, bent over, hands on knees as I gasp for air. One of the women makes the sign of the cross but I'm too out of breath to care. Agnes, of all of them, rises to her feet and comes to my side.

"What on God's green earth are ya doing?" she asks.

Sweat burns my eyes, running long rivulets down my back. I gasp air, working my mouth to try and find enough moisture to be able to speak.

"I saw... something.... by river...." I can't say more; I'm totally out of breath.

"Saw what?" Agnes asks as the other women come around.

They press in close, making it harder to catch my breath. It feels like they're stealing all the oxygen with the pressure of their looming bodies.

"A woman, in white," I say, forcing myself to stand up straight. I square my shoulders, huff another breath, then meet Agnes' narrowed eyes.

"What kind of woman in white?" Agnes asks.

The pressure of the women's presence ratchets up to eleven. It's palpable against my skin, a great weight pushing in on me from all around. I glance around to look at their suspicious eyes. I shouldn't be telling them this. I should go to Alesoun first. I've screwed up.

"Nothing. I need to get to Alesoun," I say.

"Do nae say was nothin'," Agnes snaps. "What did the woman look like? What was she doing? What were you doing?"

"I was gathering berries and came across a river where I—"

"Was she washing cloth?" Agnes interrupts.

"Yeah," I say, eyes widening in surprise. How does she already know? "And the river was—"

"Red," Agnes interrupts again. "Blood red."

I nod.

Agnes is as pale as the woman in white's dress. Her hands flutter up around her face then clench under her chin. She closes her eyes and mutters something I can't hear then makes the sign of the cross. The rest of the women mimic the gesture.

"What? Who was she? How did you know?"

"Do you nae know anything?" one of the women I don't know asks harshly.

"She's an outlander," Agnes says. "What do they know of the Highlands? Nothing. She knows nothing."

"Please," I beg. "I don't understand. I've never felt so... cold. So afraid."

"You're lying," another woman says, pointing her swollen finger and wagging it under my nose. "Liar."

Shock is like cold water in the face. The vehemence of the woman is surprising. They've never been so hateful, not directly.

"I'm not—"

"Ya are," Agnes agrees. "Ya may or may nae be a witch. I do nae know, but I do think you're a spy for the Colquhouns."

"What? No! They tried to rape me. I'd never help them. Why are you all being like this? I didn't do anything wrong."

"If'n you're nae a spy, then you're a witch. Fae touched, or I'm nae a follower of the Christ," a different woman says.

Agnes' eyes narrow with suspicion. She purses her mouth. She's thinking hard. Too hard. If she would only intervene on my behalf, they'd all stop. She's the one they all follow.

"I'm not a witch or a spy," I say.

"Aye, well then what do ya think a spy would say? They tried to rape you? Right, it was probably all arranged to capture the attention of our men folk."

"Right enough it was a setup. Look at the way she's captured Duncan's attention," another woman says.

"Agnes, please," I beg her to make this stop.

Agnes shakes her head.

"I don't know if you're a spy," Agnes says and the crowd falls silent, "but I do nae trust ya. If'n you saw what you say you did..."

She trails off, shaking her head.

"I don't even know what it was or what it's supposed to mean."

"It's a Bean Nighe. And if'n you're nae lying," Agnes says, "it means death is coming to the clan."

"Death is coming?" I shake my head as the pressure inside my chest turns to a cold front that makes me shiver.

Numbness fills my head and spreads across my limbs. It reaches my tongue, and I lose the power of speech.

"Aye," Agnes says. "So you're a liar or a witch. Either way, blood is going to be spilled. Only question is whose."

The way she looks at me, I'm not sure she's not considering sacrificing mine, right here and right now.

Chapter Twenty-One

ALESOUN and I break our fast in uncomfortable silence. She has barely spoken to me since Agnes accused me, again, of being a witch. Or a spy, because that's oh-so-much better. I barely touch my gruel. My stomach is a tight knot that refuses even the idea of food. Instead of eating, I push the white mush around with my wooden spoon.

Alesoun eats, smacking her lips with each mouthful. The scraping of her spoon on the bottom of the bowl grates on my nerves. The muscles of my shoulders tighten until I'm hunched over the table and glaring at the taunting food.

"You're nae eating," Alesoun says, rising from the table.

"I'm not hungry," I say.

She grabs my bowl without a word and returns my portion to the pot by the fire. My back and shoulders are locked so I sit, staring at the empty table. The wood is stained dark and smooth from use. The swirls of the grain almost make pictures. Like staring into the flames of a campfire. I can almost see designs and shapes that feel like they have some meaning if only I can somehow open my mind enough to understand.

Alesoun busies herself around the house in relative silence. She gets pottery jars out and places them and other items on the table until at last she sets the partial basket of berries I gathered yesterday down in front of me.

"Enough your moping," Alesoun says. "We've work to do."

"Right." I force myself onto my feet with what feels like the most extreme effort of will I've ever had to put out.

What choice do I have? I'm here. Lost. Alone. This icy cold blackness that lies over my thoughts and spirit? It's fear. Pure, unadulterated, cold fear that pushes me towards inactivity. As if, maybe, I don't move, don't act, if I lie absolutely still, all this will go away. Like I might wake up back in my own time, at home, and all of this was some drug induced dream. Or maybe something happened and I'm in a coma and this has all been some weird product of my unconsciousness.

Alesoun directs me on how to mix the ingredients to make a dough with short, harsh sounding commands. Everything has a definitive, dream-like quality to it. It doesn't feel real. None of this does. As my hands move, working the dough, it's as if time drags and the motions stutter. Like I'm in a movie and the frames are slowed down to where the actors jump from one position to the next, not bothering with the in-between movements.

A heavy weight is crushing me. I can't escape. I'm not supposed to be here, stuck with these people who are rushing towards a doom that they don't comprehend. Here I am, knowing what's coming, but I can't tell them and I can't stop it.

I'm helpless.

The thought crashes into my head like a meteor intent on destruction. There is no other way to describe this feeling and it terrifies me.

Focus. One thing at a time. One breath. One exhale.

I knead the dough, accepting Alesoun's critique on how I'm doing it without speaking. If I can't change what's coming, then I'll have to accept it. Tonight, I'll meet the dark stranger who knows more than he should. One way or another, tonight I'm getting answers.

I smile at that thought. He obviously knows more than he has said and I'm going to get him to tell me what is going on. Stress drains from my body like rain running off a slanted roof and as it goes, peace flows in behind it.

Who doesn't love some good old answers?

"Good," Alesoun says. "Now put that bowl in that cabinet to let it prove."

I do as directed, and when I've turned back around she has laid out vegetables for me to chop. This I do know how to do, so I set about the work.

"How do you do it?" I ask, concentrating on my knife work but needing to get out of my own head.

"Do what?"

"Live outside the social network. The way they treat you, keeping you at a distance. How do you do it?"

Alesoun doesn't answer. She is behind me working on something in the cabinet. When the silence stretches, I look up. She isn't working any more but standing staring into it.

"Alesoun?"

"We all have our sins," she says softly. "It's best to tend to your own and let others tend to theirs."

"That's not true. We should help each other."

"Oh, so you know better than Our Lord and Savior, do ya?" she snaps, whirling around. Her eyes are wide and her face flushed crimson. "Tis best to mind your manners, lass, or you'll end up without even my support."

"I'm sorry," I stammer, taken aback. "I didn't mean to offend."

"Ya never do, do ya? Have I nae told ya to keep your mouth shut? Did I nae warn ya? I tried to tell ya to nae antagonize them."

Her anger cuts sharper than the knife in my hands. She's my one friend, my one ally and I can't keep myself from crying. The tears leave cold trails down my cheeks, staining my lips with their salty remains. Alesoun is so angry, more than I've ever seen. I don't even know what I did to make her so. All I wanted was to help.

"I'm sorry."

I drop the knife and run out of the house.

"Quinn—" She calls after me, but I cut her off by slamming the door to her house.

I run around the corner and up into the highlands. I don't want to stand where the other women of the village can see me crying. My one ally, and I've made her mad at me too. I don't stop until I'm out of direct sight of the village. Only then do I give into the stitch in my side.

Balling my hands into fists, I shake them impotently at the sky and scream, giving voice to my frustration. Breathless, out of tears, and feeling nothing but emptiness and a crushing weight, I drop to my knees and bow my head. I offer up all my hopes and desires to whatever or whoever might be listening.

I don't know what to do. Help me. Please.

A cool breeze tugs at my hair as it chills my skin. It whistles softly as it moves through the tall grass and heather, carrying the full, rich scents. The sky is gray and cloudy and a drop of rain plops onto my bent neck, making me shiver.

"You're going to freeze to death," Duncan says, surprising me.

I jump up with a yelp.

"Sorry." He holds his hands up in surrender, standing ten feet away. "I did nae mean to startle you. Though I seem to do it often enough."

"Why are you here?" I snap.

"The entire village is talking about the crazy witch who ran into the highlands. Had to come see for myself." He grins.

"Oh, right. The crazy witch. Great. Another layer to the tale of how I'm anything but a lonely girl stuck in this living hell with a bunch of superstitious, backwater, unappreciative, judgmental jerks!"

Duncan stares for a long moment then a smile breaks across his face and he laughs. His laugh is rich and wonderful.

"Been holding that back a bit 'ave ya?"

My anger doesn't want to give way, not yet, but it's hard to stay mad when he's smiling and laughing, especially because of the way his eyes sparkle as he moves closer.

"Yes," I say, and he laughs harder. "Stop it. Don't make fun of me."

"I am nae," he says, coming a step too close. "But you are right pretty when you're angry."

The scent of him is heady, musky, but with heavy hints of animal and hay. I turn away, nursing what's left of my anger. It's not him I'm angry at; it's myself. My own inability to change the outcome of what I know is coming.

My impotence to make sure this man, whom I feel for, doesn't die. How do I save him?

That's not even considering I don't belong here. Agnes is right; he should be with a woman who does belong here. Who can stay at his side, care for him, and give him children.

Kids? Jumping the gun much there, Quinn?

"You are," I say, shaking my head. "Don't bother denying it. I know how you men are."

"Oh, do ya now? Have us menfolk all figured out, huh?"

He places one hand on the small of my back and it is electric. That simple touch instigates a summer storm that rages through my nervous system. Every inch of my skin tingles, alert and alive, demanding attention. His attention. He pushes gently until we're walking together. He leads the way over to the rock outcropping where he takes a seat.

"I do," I answer at last. "Deceitful. Always with an agenda."

"Deceitful, am I?"

"Aye," I say, and can't stop a smile from spreading across my face as I use the familiar Scottish acknowledgment.

"Well," he says, "I would tend to disagree, but how would I prove my lack of deceit?"

"I don't know. I mean, if you are lying, wouldn't you lie about lying?"

"Hmm, a complex problem."

We stare into each other's eyes. The setting sun casts rosy gold rays that have fought their way through the heavy gray clouds above to impale us on their fading glory.

"Indeed," I say, leaning closer without meaning to. He has a gravity that pulls me in and won't let me go.

"Perhaps if I were to swear to ya, on my mother's grave, I have never and will never lie to you."

He speaks with such sincerity it rings in my ears and echoes in my soul. Our mouths are so close, the warmth of his breath caresses my lips and cheeks.

"Perhaps," I whisper, afraid the sound of my voice will break the moment.

"Then I do."

"Do?"

"I do so swear. I have never nor will I ever lie to you."

"Even if it hurts me?"

"I would nae enjoy it, but no, I will nae lie."

The lies I've told him scorch my heart. I want to tell him everything, to be honest with him, but he would never believe me. And if he did, what then? He would never accept me. A sharp, hot pain stabs into my chest.

Why does that realization make me hurt so badly?

"Let me start by saying something that has been on my mind since I first laid eyes on ya."

I swallow hard, unable to take my eyes off his. "What?"

"You are the most beautiful woman God above has ever allowed to walk on the Earth."

"Flattery."

"Flattery is a lie, dressed up in niceness. It is not flattery. It is the truth."

My lips touch his. A spark jumps between them, numbing mine, but the warm softness of his soothes the ache. His mouth moves on mine as the cool highland breeze blows across us. His arms enclose my body, pulling me closer.

Damn it. I'm falling. Falling into him.

Falling in love.

Chapter Twenty-Two

HIS KISS FEELS NATURAL, as if this is what we've always been meant to do. All our interaction before this kiss, even the last time he kissed me, was only a preamble to this. In some strange way, it is as if we've been locked in some time-travelling, millennia-long foreplay. Having done this before and knowing we'll do it again in time.

When at last he pulls back, we're both panting. I stare into his gorgeous eyes, losing myself in them. He sees me. The real me, beyond the facade I present to the world.

"Duncan," I say, touching his cheek. His stubble is rough and poky, but I like it. "I have to tell you something. Will you listen? Please?"

"Ya make it sound right serious."

"It is. Deadly serious but I need you to listen. Hear me out."

"Aye, of course." He smiles easily.

"This proclamation, from the King—"

"Ach, don't worry yourself about that. We'll handle it."

"No, you won't," I say. "It's bad. Worse than you can possibly imagine."

"Quinn, I know it seems scary but ya can't let fear grip ya, lass.

We've been to war before. We'll go to war again. It does nae matter but I'll tell you true, we will nae allow the Colquhouns or those bastard Campbells to manipulate us or steal our lands. Not again."

"Again?"

"Aye." He nods. "They tricked us out of our rightful lands once before. Alisdair will nae allow it again. We'll be fine. We're smarter than they are."

I close my eyes and swallow hard, trying to force the lump in my throat back down to wherever it came from. He's so confident, cocky even, and I like it. Certainty is always attractive in a man, but in this case he's wrong. Dead wrong.

"You promised to listen," I say, reminding him.

"Aye, lass, go ahead."

He shuts his mouth and sits in silence while I try to collect my thoughts enough to say what I want to say and not sound crazy. Which is a much harder task than it has any right to be.

"It's going to be bad. You must believe me when I tell you, it's going to be so awful they're going to—" I cut myself off from saying that his name itself will be banished. "They'll not only kill the men. They'll kill your families, women, children even. There has to be some way to stop this."

"Quinn, ya can't know all that. No one can know the future, lass. It's nae possible."

This is it. I should shut my mouth now. Figure out some other way, but how? I can't not tell him. He'll listen. He feels for me too; I'm sure he does.

"I do know. I *know!*" I blurt out.

His face darkens and he pulls back.

"No. You cannae. It's not possible. Don't ya realize it's talk like this that keeps ya on the outs with the other womenfolk? They hear ya talkin' like this and that's why they're thinking you're a witch."

As he speaks, frustration builds in my chest. The pressure increases with every word he says until it erupts into anger.

"What of it?" I snap. If this is what it takes to get him to help stop this, then so be it. They want a witch; I'll give them a witch. "I do know and if that makes me a 'witch' or whatever you want to label me, then I am. Fine."

"Quinn, you're nae being yourself."

I try to stand and almost fall as my feet tangle in the long skirt. Duncan leaps up and catches me, keeping me from falling, but I jerk free of his hands.

"How would you know?"

I glare, daring him to challenge me. He stares, thoughts racing across his face as plain as day, then at last he shrugs.

"I know you," he says. He pauses, takes a deep breath, then shakes his head. "I cannae pretend to understand, but I feel like I've always known ya. Forever like."

"Me too," I say in a hoarse whisper.

We stare at each other for a long time. My heart thumps in my chest as he takes my hands in his. His hands are rough and warm, and a small part of me wants to feel those hands all over my body.

"Ya have to stop this," he says, a note of pleading to his voice. "You're scared. That's fine, but ya cannae be saying things like this. Trust me, it will all be fine."

It won't and I know it. I'm standing at a crossroads. I can keep my secret, keep my mouth shut, and walk away. Except if I do that, then he might die. Some of these people I've come to know will for sure.

I can't. I can't leave it.

"It won't," I whisper, looking up and meeting his eyes. I clear my throat and blink away my tears. "I *know*. I can't tell you how, but you have to believe me. I know and it's bad. I can't tell everyone, but you can. Advise Chief Johnne, convince him to not go to war. You have to."

"Quinn, you're talking as if ya really are a witch."

"What if I am? Does it matter? Does it change the way you feel about me? 'Cause I'm telling you, I feel the same about you. I do but you must believe me. I know this is bad."

"How? How can ya know?"

I chew my lip, trying to come up with an answer that makes sense. I have to convince him so I lean into the one thing that might work.

"Sometimes, I get glimpses of the future," I say. "I see bits and pieces. I know things."

"Quinn..." He says my name, letting his voice trail off. He looks away, not meeting my eyes, then he makes the sign of the cross. My stomach roils, forcing acid to burn a painful path up my throat. "Only the Devil can grant ya sight of the future. Is that what your—"

"Or the fae," I interject.

He stops, staring at me, then he nods slowly and drops my hands. My arms hang heavily at my sides. I don't have the strength to lift them on my own.

"I'm going back now," he says and turns his back.

"Duncan!" I yell. "Please. You have to believe me."

"No," he says without turning around. "I do nae. If'n you're smart as I believe ya to be, you'll keep this to yourself. Do nae be spreading your words around."

He strides away, leaving me alone on the highlands. My heart shatters with each step away he takes.

Chapter Twenty-Three

ALONE AND HEARTBROKEN, I stare down the empty path. Duncan is gone and no matter it's for the best, I'm alone and it hurts. I have no right to feel this way, no right to capture his attention, I don't belong here. Heavy drops of cold rain splat on my head. Shivering, I consider going back to the village, but I can't face Duncan. Turning my back on the path I wander, waiting for dark.

The rain never develops and soon the clouds part. As the sun sets, the vast sky—twinkling with millions of stars I don't think I've ever seen so clearly—mocks me with its black emptiness. Those dots of sparkling light are like my hope: so incredibly far away they're not really real.

The moon emerges from the clouds casting its cold, silvery light on the land. I rub my face to force blood flow and drive back the numbing cold. As the moon comes fully out, its pure white face stares, sitting in impassive judgment.

The world around me has an air of unreality, as if I've stepped into a negative dimension. All the landmarks are here, the same, but colored in black, white, and silver. Clouds move across the moon, creating shadows that chase each other through the grass and across the stone outcrops.

I make my way towards the standing stone and as I do, resolve becomes certainty. Tonight, I'm getting answers. No more mystery. No more clever ploys. If I have to shake it out of the dark stranger, I'm getting the truth.

Certainty breeds confidence and they join in my heart. I square my shoulders and lengthen my stride. I don't know how to handle Duncan or save this village, but if anyone is to have a clue, it's the stranger. This isn't for me alone anymore. The lives of the villagers hang in the balance. It doesn't matter that many of them have been mean or treated me like an outcast; none of them deserve to die.

The standing stone where he said to meet comes into view. The moon shines its full light down on it and creates an empty pool of silvery-white around it. I stop and look around, trying to spot him.

"If you don't show up, I'm going to..." I mutter, walking ahead faster.

Going to what? Yell? Shake my fists in the air? What exactly am I going to do?

It's not like I have a clue how to fight. I've never been in a physical confrontation in my life. It doesn't matter; none of my negative thoughts are enough to damage my resolve. I'm going to do something. What, I'll figure that out when I'm in front of his stupid, know-it-all face.

The standing stone casts a long shadow as I climb towards it. As I get closer, there's still no sign of him.

"You son of a—"

"Quinn," he says, stepping out from behind the stone.

I bite back a yelp, my heart racing. I could see everything as I approached, and he wasn't there a moment ago.

"How did you do that?"

He answers with a smile. Something flutters and then a raven, or maybe it's the raven, lands on top of the stone behind him. The raven caws then tilts its head and stares.

"And why is that bird following me?"

"You showed up," he says.

"That's not an answer," I say, crossing my arms over my chest and glaring. I wait for a response but neither he nor the stupid bird say anything. Those aren't the important questions anyway. "What choice do I have?"

"Quinn, there is always a choice and the choice is always yours."

I close the distance between us in two long strides. He's taller than I am, forcing me to crane my neck back and look up at him. He must be six four, maybe six five. His face is no longer hidden in shadow. He's darker than I expected for some reason. He's also stunningly good looking, which blasts away the snappy comeback I had prepared.

"You..."

The rest of the thought is gone.

"Yes, I am me. You are you," he says.

I shake my head and think of Duncan. Of how mean I've been to him while he has been so nice. Of how I've had to keep him at a distance because I don't belong here. Of all the questions I have.

This guy has the answer I need and like that, I find my resolve.

"I want answers."

"You always do."

"That! You said 'always'. What does that even mean? You act like you've known me all my life or something. I'm sure I would remember you if that was true. Why do you make statements like that?"

He purses his lips, and I can't help but notice how plush and full they are. I bet he's a good kisser. Those lips demand kissing. Worse, the same sensation I get with Duncan is there. A teasing at the corners of my thoughts, that feeling I've known him for years.

I shake my head, trying to clear it of the stupid inane thoughts.

He looks past me, staring off into the distance. I turn my head to try and see what he's looking at but there's nothing but empty grass.

"No," he says.

"No? No, what?"

My pulse throbs in my temple as my blood pressure shoots up. A slow, cold smile forms and he shakes his head.

"No. It means negative. It means that I won't answer your questions. Yet."

"You won't? Then why did you bring me here? What is the point of this? How do I get home?"

"You ask the wrong questions."

"Fine. How do I stop this? How do I save them?"

"Them?"

I wave my hand behind me towards the village.

He smiles and shakes his head. "I'm sorry, wrong question."

"Great. So how am I supposed to figure out the right questions?"

"You always do." He sighs. "Sooner or later."

"Enough," I yell, clenching my hands tight. My nails dig into the palms and I'm sure they must be drawing blood. "Tell me how I got here. Tell me how to get home. If you can't do that then tell me how I can save him."

Damn it, that last bursts out of my mouth without thinking. Him. Duncan. It's a truth that resonates like a gong in my soul. Damn it. I said more than I should have.

His smile becomes sardonic.

"You can't," he says. "Come, walk with me."

He offers his hand. I glare at it, waiting for him to say something more. The moment stretches uncomfortably but he doesn't move. I don't even see him blink. He waits, patient as the standing stone behind him. Time is a thing that doesn't matter to him in the slightest.

"No."

He doesn't react and doesn't move. His extended hand hangs between us as if it's frozen in place. Frozen in time and waiting.

"Seriously?" I ask.

"I do not understand. Am I serious about what I'm telling you? Or am I serious about asking you to walk with me?"

"Yes, to both of them."

"Then yes, I am serious. Please. Come with me. It is easier to show you than to tell."

"Show me what?"

"Exactly."

It feels like my body temperature is rising with each statement he makes. If he keeps going, my blood is going to be boiling me from the inside out. He has answers. I need answers. I've come this far; I might as well play along.

"Fine," I say and take his hand.

His hand is cool, almost cold, and dry, but it sparks familiarity. As if I've held his hand many times and know its shape, its feeling well. He leads us towards the standing stone. A mist rises from the ground, growing thicker with each step. Fear makes my heart flutter.

"What is happening?"

He doesn't answer. He looks like he's concentrating, his lips moving. I don't hear words or any sound, but the mist becomes a heavy fog. My heart races as the fog rises. It's up to my waist and still coming.

"Stop!" I yell. "Stop this. Are you taking me home? I can't leave yet. What is happening?"

My head is barely above the fog. He stands head and shoulders above it as I look around, terrified. I try to jerk my hand out of his, but his grip tightens painfully.

"You're hurting me. Let me go."

He continues muttering, pulling me along beside him. We're still moving towards the stone; the tip of it is the last thing I see before the fog covers my head.

Chapter Twenty-Four

WHITE FOG SURROUNDS US, so thick I can't see my hand in front of my face. It's chilly, wet, cloying, and making me claustrophobic. Fear thrums in every muscle. My only point of certainty is the dark stranger's hand.

"Do not fear," he says, his voice dull and muffled. "We are almost there."

"Almost where? Where are you taking me?"

"To your destiny."

"Because that's an answer," I say. "You practice this whole cryptic stranger thing?"

The fog thins and then we step out. As we break free, the fog clings to us like it's trying to keep us from getting away from its cold white grip. We're not where we were but this also isn't home.

A huge white ash tree dominates my field of vision. It fills the night with massive branches that stretch across the sky. The tree seems to emit a light of its own. A soft, white-silver glow that outlines every leaf. My breath catches in my throat as I stumble to a stop.

"I've seen this before," I whisper.

"Yes," my guide says.

I close my eyes and take a deep breath. The air is rich with the scent of the sea, salt, and fish layering over the thickness of fresh heather. I open my eyes and look at the stranger.

"Who are you?"

He does a slow blink.

"Call me Dugald," he says at last.

"Okay, Dugald, where are we? Why have you brought me here and how do I get home?"

"You are home," he says, then walks away.

"Hey," I yell at his back, rushing to catch up to him. "This isn't home. I don't know where this is."

He has long legs and it's all I can do to try and keep up to him. He heads towards the tree, and I follow. Small, rough buildings made from woven branches and stacked rocks dot the landscape as we come under the branches of the tree.

People move about, tending to whatever business they are doing. I focus on catching up to Dugald, not paying much attention to anyone or anything else until something I half-see in my peripheral vision causes me to stop.

A young boy, who can't be more than twelve or thirteen, with reddish-brown curly hair and a cherubic face, is crouched by a fire. What stops me in my tracks is his antlers. They protrude from the sides of his head as natural as a deer, but he's a boy. He sees me staring and stands up, dusting his tattered, rough spun pants at the knees.

"Hi," he says, walking over and offering his hand.

"Uhm, hi," I say, taking his offered hand.

"Are you here with Dug?"

"Uh, yeah, I think so."

"You think or you know?"

"I know," I correct. "Yeah, with him."

"Come along," Dugald says, appearing beside me and gripping my arm.

"She's being friendly, Dug," the deer-boy says.

159

"I do not have time for friendly, Cernunnos," Dugald says. "You know this."

"You have as much time as you allot," Cernunnos says with an easy grin.

Dugald snorts, pulling me away.

"It was nice to meet you," I say over my shoulder.

"Again," Cernunnos says.

"Huh?" I ask but Dugald pulls harder on my arm, and I have to pay attention to where I'm walking or risk falling.

"Ignore him," Dugald says.

"Why?" I ask, looking around with rampant curiosity.

None of the people we pass are, well, people. They're not human, or not wholly human. I can't look around fast enough or process what I see quick enough to make sense of any one thing. I see kids who look like old people dressed in leaves. People who are hybrids with animals of all kinds. And then I see the fairies.

The fairies are tiny people with translucent wings that shimmer as they dart about the branches of the tree. The sound of tinkling bells fills the air as they pass as though they are wearing them hidden in their clothing. Or maybe that's just the sound their wings make as they fly; I can't tell.

"Where are we?" I ask.

"Finally, a good question," Dugald grumbles.

"You don't have to be mean."

"No matter what any here tell you," he says, "we do not have time."

"And that is not an answer," I counter.

"You are in the Fae realm," he says.

"It's beautiful."

We're close to the trunk of the tree. It's as big as a building. I don't think twenty men could link their arms around it. Veins of silver trace their way up and down the trunk and the entire area is bathed in the light of the tree. I'm reminded of the story told by the bard back at the village.

Under the tree boughs, we stand in the middle of a village that rises from and blends in with the natural surroundings. The different creatures talk and work. There's a surreal quality to everything, as if all of this is nothing more than a dream.

"Is it?" he asks.

"What do you mean?"

"Look, Quinn. Really look."

I don't understand what he wants, but I do as he commands. I look, picking out a fairy who's flitting between the leaves of a low branch. It's a beautiful, tiny girl. She wears a tiny leaf that is tied around her waist and her long, luscious brown hair almost magically keeps her breasts covered. She touches each leaf and as she does it slightly dims. Then she moves to the next one and the same thing happens again.

Something about her though is off. I look harder, squinting, and her perfect skin isn't quite so perfect. Her lush hair is actually lank. Even the tree itself, now that I look, isn't as bright as it seems.

"What is this?" I ask, walking towards the tree.

When I'm close enough, I touch it. My fingers tingle. Gentle energy flows to me from it. The bark is smooth and lined with silvery veins that pulse. But as I look closer, I see flaws. The veins of silver dim out in places. The bark is rough in areas. Between some of the folds of the bark is darkness, and a black ooze seeps out.

"Rot," Dugald says.

"Rot?" I ask, reaching towards the ooze.

"No!" Dugald knocks my hand down.

I cry out, rubbing my forearm where he struck me. "Why did you do that?"

"Never touch the rot. Never."

"Fine," I grumble. "What are you trying to show me? This isn't home. If you can't get me home, then you need to help me help the MacGregors. They're going to die. I need your help to save them."

"We can't," he says.

"Why not? You've got... magic or whatever. You're what, fae? Like they keep accusing me of. Alesoun said I'm fae-touched. How do I help them?"

Dugald frowns and shakes his head, his face darkening. "That is not your destiny."

"Not my destiny? I don't believe in destiny."

Duncan fills my thoughts. The scent of him. His smile. His easy manner. Then I think of Alesoun and how nice she has been to me. I can't let them die. I know how bad it's going to be for them. Worse than anything they've ever experienced.

"A genocide is coming, and I know it. I'm here, impossibly so. How can it be that it's not my destiny or whatever to stop this?"

"Ask fate. I do not know," he says. "All I can tell you is you can't stop it."

"Then what is my destiny, as you call it?"

"To save us," he says.

It's as if the entire world around us stops. All the different fae folk stare at me with eyes filled with hope, but their faces show despair. I turn in a slow circle as I choke up, my throat clenching as tight as my stomach which is queasy.

"Wh—what?" I force the single word past the lump.

He doesn't answer but only stares at me too. I shake my head and swallow, focusing on breathing until my clenched muscles ease enough I can speak.

"You can't be serious."

"I am not known for my sense of humor," he says.

"Really? You've been such a riot."

He moves in closer. Too close. He dominates the space, stealing the air from my lips. He leans over, forcing me to strain my neck. His face is stern, but handsome. He leans down and my lips tremble. I think, for a moment, he's going to kiss me and oddly enough, I want him to.

"You are our only hope." He exhales, his breath unnaturally cool, like a fresh mint.

"I'm no one."

"Wrong."

I tremble, stuck between an insane desire to kiss him and an urge to run. I step back but I come up against the tree, its rough bark pressing into my skin, pinning me here, in this moment, with him.

"Help me save the MacGregors."

"No."

"No? Why? You can?"

"We can't. That history is written. Immutable."

"Then how am I supposed to save you?"

"It's your world that is killing us. You, your new generation, have lost the ability to dream. Your dreams are being force fed to you by flashing screens and moving images. Your kind don't think. They seek out numbness, retreat into drug fueled madness."

"And what exactly am I supposed to do about that?"

"Change it."

"How?"

"I'm not the One. That's on you."

"And if I refuse?"

He frowns and steps back. I take in what feels like the first breath I've had since he closed in.

"Then you're no better than the rest of your kind."

"And what does that mean?" I ask, pushing off the tree and stepping up to him. "You got some kind of smart response? What am I supposed to do here? I've been yanked out of my time, stuck in the past, and the people I've come to call friends are about to have their entire world destroyed. Most, if not all of them, are probably going to die and you want me to, what? Not care? Walk away and come help you do god knows what?"

"Yes," he says. "That is exactly what I expect."

"Then you can piss right off. Help me save the MacGregors."

"You don't listen."

"I do listen. You want my help? Help me back."

He spins on one heel, takes one step, and he's gone. Everyone that was staring at our confrontation resumes what they were doing as if nothing happened. As if I don't exist.

I turn a circle looking for him. He's gone.

Chapter Twenty-Five

ANGER BURNS through my body and surges with the pounding of my heart. I shake with frustration, trying to wrap my head around how Dugald can be such a jerk. What am I supposed to do now?

I close my eyes and count to ten, and at last the anger recedes. Now I feel burned out and alone. When I open my eyes, I'm still alone. I'd hoped maybe Dugald would return but now I'm left with nothing. I don't know where I am or what I'm supposed to do. Find my destiny. How about you kiss my butt, jerk.

"How do I get home?" I ask, turning a circle.

"Home?" asks a voice so deep it feels like it rumbles in my bones.

I look around but don't see who asked the question. None of the fae folk are that close and those that are nearby aren't paying attention to me. I look up in the tree, but don't see anyone.

"Who?"

"Down here."

When I look down, a garden gnome stands in front of me. He's under two feet tall. I blink several times to make sure I'm seeing what I think I'm seeing. I can't believe this is real. The gnome is dressed in a bright red cap that matches the color on his cheeks and has a thick white beard. Blue shirt, yellow pants, and brown boots. He's a garden gnome, except real.

"Hello," I say, smiling and trying to cover my embarrassment at not speaking sooner.

"Right. You said home."

"Uhm, yes. I need to get home."

He narrows his eyes. "What are you willing to do for it?"

"What do you mean?"

"Everything has a price. What price will you pay for it?"

"Don't you do it," a high-pitched female voice says right next to my ear.

Floating in the air next to me is one of the small fairies I saw darting around the leaves earlier. She has silvery hair that floats around her head almost like a halo.

She wags her finger at the gnome. "She's not here to make deals with the likes of you. You let her be."

"Bah," the gnome says. "She asked."

"And you can go on your way. Now," the fairy says.

The gnome grumbles but turns and stomps away. Puffs of dirt poof with each pounding of his feet.

"Thank you," I say, unsure what else to say.

"You don't know what you're doing," the fairy says, flitting up and down like a hummingbird darting between flowers. "You don't want to make deals with him. He'll hold you to the letter and that's never good. Don't trust him."

"Okay," I say. "But I do need to get back."

"Back is a state of mind. Maybe you need to go forward," she says. She talks as fast as her wings are moving, a mile a minute.

"Maybe?"

"Dugald brought you," she says as a statement. "We've been waiting for you. If he's right, you're the one. Or you could not be the one. You could be a deceiver."

"I don't think I'm the one anything."

166

"Isn't that what the one would think? Yes. Yes, I think it is. If the one thought they were the one, then what would be the point of being the one? They'd be too full of themselves to be the one."

I'm having trouble keeping up with her train of thought, which is circuitous enough on its own, but the speed she talks is ridiculous.

"Okay, can you help me?"

"Of course I can. Any of us can. Depending what it is you need help with there will be someone here who can help. For now at least. Soon we won't be able to help anyone. We can't help ourselves, of course. If we could, we wouldn't need you, now would we?"

I blink and shake my head. "Sure."

"You need to see Caill. She's the one for you."

"Where do I find her?"

She points in a direction and then she frowns and points in the opposite direction. "Good luck."

She smiles and flitters off.

"But—!"

She's gone. I turn in a circle, sucking in a breath. No one is paying any particular attention to me. The different creatures do their work and only once in a while do I catch any of them so much as casting a glance in my direction.

Never mind the stranger lost in your midst.

Something moves towards me, coming into my peripheral vision fast. I duck, throwing my arms up for protection. A bird flies over my head then it caws loudly. Straightening, I turn around and see the raven sitting on one of the tree limbs. It tilts its head, one beady eye staring, and caws, opening and closing its wings.

"You are a jerk," I growl, and it bobs its head as if in agreement.

The raven's wings flutter then it lifts into the air and flies over my head again. I duck and turn with it as it passes. It flies in a circle as if waiting. I look around in a vain hope that someone else, anyone else, will offer some help or advice but no, I'm left to follow the bird.

Sighing, I do. It pauses fifty feet ahead and circles, apparently waiting for me to follow it. I have my doubts about this but having no other options, I follow. It stops every fifty feet or so and circles, making sure I'm with it, then resumes flying. It leads me past the tiny huts, out of the marketplace setting, and towards the dark that lies at the edge of the tree's branches.

An undefinable ache forms in my guts when I look too long at that darkness. There's a wrongness to the shadowy dark. The closest I can define it is a sense of dread. It's the dark of a partially open closet when I was a child where I know there was a monster waiting for me to stop looking. Or the shadows under the bed, keeping me from climbing out all night, no matter how bad I needed to use the bathroom. This dark seems to swirl and move almost like it's breathing.

I look over my shoulder as we come to what seems like the edge of the fae village, barely under the edge of the tree's branches. The light it casts is dim and has a slight flicker, like a fluorescent bulb that is at the end of its life.

The raven's cry echoes through my head, pulling my attention back to where the bird sits on a ramshackle building. It's not a big building, probably not much more than a single room. Smoke rises from a bent pipe that serves as a chimney. The wood of the walls is dark with age and shows signs of rot. The door hangs crooked, and the windows are shuttered. I give the door a tentative knock. I'm afraid to find out what is inside but I don't think I have any choice.

"Come in, Quinn."

My heart hammers faster. The voice inviting me in sounds ancient. Scratchy as if it hasn't spoken in a long time or perhaps it belongs to a person who smokes. A lot. Five packs a day for years.

I grab the rusty ring that serves as a door handle and pull but the door doesn't move. I pull harder and it still doesn't move.

Finally, I plant my feet and pull as hard as I can. The door flies open. I stumble back, feeling like a fool, and the raven caws.

"Laugh it up," I mutter, glaring at the bird.

The room beyond the open door is smoky. A pot belly stove has its door open, casting an orange glow that illuminates the space. I duck my head to enter and smell the most succulent, savory scents I think I've ever inhaled. It reminds me of Christmas dinners at Grandma's, a full cornucopia of scents mixing to create a sensory feeling that I can only describe as love and home.

"Hello?"

I wave a hand in front of my face, stirring the smoke. A figure is bent over the stove, stirring something in a pot. When the person turns around, it's a bowed, old woman with a craggy face that is icy blue. She has piercing, glistening black eyes that look like they're all pupils and no other color.

"Well? Sit. Do you think I have forever to wait on you?"

She motions to a stool on one side of a table. The table is set for two. She grabs the bowl from the table and shuffles to the stove where she ladles something from the pot. It plops into the bowl like a stew.

The story that the bard told at the village fire about the lost shepherd comes to mine. Never eating food in fairy lands was the moral of the tale. Well, one of the morals. No matter how good it smells.

"Thank you," I say. "I'm not actually hungry."

"And she starts our conversation with a lie. A bold choice, eh Riki?"

I look around quickly to spot who Riki is but before I see anyone the raven caws. In the small space, his voice is even louder. It's clear that Riki is the raven.

Oh, boy.

"Sorry," I say, taking the seat.

"Hospitality," the woman says, placing a steaming bowl of

what looks like a stew in front of me. "It's important. Manners. People of your time, you've lost all sense of them. Terrible."

The raven caws its agreement with her assessment. I pick up a wooden spoon and stir.

"Are you Caill?"

"Sometimes I am," she says, "though shortening a person's name like that is rude. You are every bit as rude and obnoxious as I expected."

"I'm not," I protest.

"I'm not," Caill mimics and the raven caws as if it's laughing along with her. "Let me refuse your hospitality, butcher your name, and the next thing she'll ask is how to get home. Care to bet?"

"What else am I supposed to ask?"

"You don't listen, do you Quinn? How many times has Dugald told you to ask the right questions? How many times have you not listened? Not looked?"

"I don't understand," I say.

"No, you don't," she says, taking the seat opposite with her own bowl of stew.

She hunches over the bowl as if protecting it from someone that might seek to snatch it. No matter how good it smells, my stomach is clenched too tight to accept any food. I continue stirring to try and hide the fact I'm not eating.

"He said I have a destiny."

"Yes. You do."

"What is it?"

"You are the Destroyer."

A cold hand slowly closes around my chest, chilling me to the bone. I stop stirring, but I'm not going to pretend to eat. Caill continues shoveling the food into her mouth making disgusting slurping and smacking sounds as she barely chews before shoveling the next bite in.

"Excuse me?"

Caill stops eating. She stares at her bowl for four beats of my heart before slowly, so slowly it feels like her head is being dragged up, raising her eyes to mine.

"You. Rude girl. Are the Destroyer."

"Destroyer of what?"

"Finally, she asks a good question, eh?"

The raven caws.

"It depends, doesn't it? You will destroy, but what, hmm? See, value in a good question."

"I don't want to destroy anything."

"Sure, sure. They all say that. I don't want to be what I am. I'll deny myself but nature is nature. You will do what you will do and, in the end, it will be by your will and you will destroy."

"That doesn't make sense. I've never destroyed anything in my life."

"Haven't you?" She locks her dark eyes onto mine and my heart stops.

Fear is a dark cloud filling my head. I don't want to hear what she's going to say next. I know with every fiber of my being that I don't want to know.

I shake my head.

"Then I'm wrong," Caill sighs. "You're not the Destroyer. You're the Fool. Sooner or later, you'll fulfill your role, but not yet it seems."

She resumes consuming her food. I'm left cold with aching muscles that refuse to unclench. I force my jaw to relax then my shoulders and take a deep breath.

"I need to get home," I say.

"And there it is, eh Riki?" She snorts. "When it's time."

"When is that?"

"Want to know a funny thing about time?"

"Uhm, sure."

"It doesn't care." She laughs, a raucous cackle that sounds suspiciously like a raven cawing.

"That's not funny."

"Huh, depends on your viewpoint, because it really is. You humans. I want this. I want that. I can't wait. I need it now. What? Wait a week to receive a package? Too slow? Overnight? Too slow. Instant. I want it now. An entire generation of mewling humans demanding to be satisfied now."

"What are you talking about?"

"You!" she says, exploding to her feet so fast her bowl flies off the table and clangs against the potbelly stove.

I recoil in horror, leaning back and covering myself with my arms.

"All of your kind. Your entire generation. Worthless."

She turns her back and shuffles to a corner. I watch her, ready to flee at the first sign of violence. I may not have anywhere to go but I can sure not be here. She lifts a bucket from the floor with a grunt. She shuffles back to the table and stops, setting the bucket on the ground beside the table and panting.

"Do you need—"

Her glare cuts me off before I finish the thought and I drop back onto my chair.

She grabs the bucket with both hands, huffs loudly, then lifts it up and sets it on the table. Water sloshes over the edge, splashing on the table, some of it landing in my untouched stew. I'm too scared to move, waiting to see what happens next.

"Come, come." Caill motions for me to stand up.

She leans over the bucket, and I lean in to look too. It's full of murky water but all I see is our reflections staring back. Caill puts one finger into the water and moves it slowly counterclockwise.

"What—"

She shushes me and I snap my mouth shut. The water swirls and it's no longer the reflection of our faces on the surface. I see home. High rises, cars racing down freeways, people rushing up and down a city street. All the people are on their phones and staring at the screen. No one looks up or takes notice of the other people around them. The view shifts to movie theatres with flashing lights and hundreds of staring eyes. Televisions casting flickering light over the enraptured people watching.

The point of view shifts to inside an apartment, watching a family staring at a screen but slowly pulls back. It's outside the apartment and looking in through a window. The point of view continues pulling back. More windows come into view, all with the same flickering light of televisions.

The water swirls and changes to a silver tree. The one that dominates this land of fairy. The Tree of Life; it must be just like in the story but now its light is gone. The dark shadow that made me ache when I looked at it has laid claim. It hurts me, burning like my veins are filled with lava. I can't breathe. It's wrong. So wrong. I gasp and look aways, clenching my eyes tight.

"What is this?" I ask, gritting my teeth as sweat beads on my brow.

"The future."

"But it's... awful."

"What did you expect? Fields of poppies and roses?"

"I don't know, not this. It's sad. All those people stuck to their screens."

"Aye," Caill says. "Like you."

"I'm not—"

"Now."

I open my mouth to protest but can't. She's not wrong. I was every bit as bad about keeping up on my phone. Before coming to this time, I don't remember the last time I took a moment look around. To see other people in real life. How bad is it when we even had to develop a term for it? 'In real life.' I swallow hard.

"We're dying," Caill says. "It's on you to save us or to leave us to fade away."

"What do you mean? How can it be me?"

"Look. Did you not see? Are you still blind from your tiny screens?"

I shake my head and fight the urge to cry. "I'm sorry. I don't understand."

"Foolish child," she huffs and the raven flies to her shoulder. "You are the Destroyer. Which world will you choose? Ours or the one you knew?"

"How am I supposed to choose that? I don't want to lose my friends. I don't want to lose my loved ones." *I don't want to lose Duncan. Alesoun. Robert. Patrick. Chief Johnne. All the MacGregors who have been so nice and welcoming.* "Oh my god! The MacGregors. How do I save them? They're in so much danger. I have to save them. How can I?"

She straightens, rising to her full height for the first time. In her eyes is a wintry storm and her face is cold as ice. She towers over me and the raven spreads its wings to fill the hut.

"You can't save them. It's written and done."

"No. There has to be a way. You want me to save you? Help me save them."

She motions to the bucket.

Hands trembling, unable to breathe, I look. I see a clear Scottish Highland day. The Colquhouns are gathered in force and armed to the teeth. The MacGregor army charges and at the lead of it is Duncan.

Shots are fired, puffs of smoke rising over the battlefield. Duncan, leading the charge, takes a bullet in the chest. Blood explodes in slow motion. He's lifted up and thrown backwards, dropping to the ground as others charge past him.

"No!" I scream, throwing the bucket. It flies off the table, water spilling everywhere, and clatters against the wall. "Send me back. Now. I have to save him."

The old woman leans her head back and laughs. The laugh becomes a cackle, echoing in my ears, invoking despair. Then she sets her dark gaze on me, and her tone turns grave. "You're too late."

Chapter Twenty-Six

CAILL RESUMES HER LAUGHING. She holds her sides, shaking her head and showing her yellow-brown teeth. The sound of her laugh is nails on a chalkboard. Screeching, cutting through my head, shredding at my sanity.

"Stop," I say, covering my ears in a vain attempt to block her out.

Her laughter won't be denied, piercing through my hands and driving into my eardrums like an ice pick.

The image of Duncan dying replays in my head, over and over like a movie looping in slow motion. His mouth opens and he yells his battle cry. He leads the charge and the sun glints off the edge of his claymore. Then the bullet slams into him. The spray of blood, individual droplets catching the sun's rays and dispersing tiny rainbows around each one of them. His eyes widen as his body is thrown back by the force of the bullet.

"No. No. No." I squeeze my eyes tight, clench my jaw, and ball my fists. "No."

Destiny? How can it be that my destiny is to save these fairies I don't know or save the ones I love?

Tears fall, unstoppable. A black pit swirls in my core, swal-

175

lowing everything. Something cool, yet warm touches my skin, almost as if someone is spreading menthol on me. As the icy warmth soaks in, the blackness of despair swallows the warmth, but more of the warmth pours in until at last the blackness recedes, only a little, but as it goes, I can breathe.

"Stop it," I growl.

I open my eyes and glare at Caill.

My protest only seems to fuel her amusement. She laughs harder, wiping tears of joy from her glistening eyes.

"Stop it?" She guffaws. "That's not my domain, now is it, lass? Oh no, it's not. Stop it, she demands."

The raven's cawing joins her laughter, accenting it. The sounds of their mirth fill the space with discordance. While they laugh, the coolness and the warmth reaches into my core surrounding the blackness, pressing in on it. And then the blackness compresses and becomes a hard ball.

No. I ball my hands into tight fists and grit my teeth. *No. This is no choice. There must be another way.*

Resolve coalesces and the stronger that becomes the more it presses in on the blackness. Pressure builds in my core, higher and higher. I tremble, struggling to contain it. The darkness explodes, pushing Caill back. The furniture of her home clatters as it's thrown against the walls.

"Stop!" I scream.

My voice echoes in my ears as if I'm yelling into a deep, black cave. My skin thrums as if every nerve is newly alive. Something crackles across my body, lifting every tiny hair, causing goose pimples to race along my limbs and a chill to trail down my spine. I straighten and I feel taller. Bigger. I feel as if I'm somehow more.

Caill stops laughing. Her laughter and amusement turns into a dour grimace. Her eyes widen and her mouth full of rotten teeth hangs open.

"You dare," she hisses.

She rises, impossibly tall; the room seems to expand to accommodate her but I'm becoming every bit as tall and consuming as she. The icy-blue of her face darkens towards a stormy gray, rich with an impending storm. Lightning crackles between her fingers and her eyes burn like twin flames.

I should be scared. a small, rational, part of me whispers.

I'm not. Not in the slightest. Fear is there. I know it, but only in the way I know the things in my bedroom. Aware of them but they don't require my attention and neither, in this case, does fear. I'm not even sure I'm angry. This is something beyond the simplicity of emotions.

I'm powerful. Power pours into my body. As it does, my awareness expands. I'm more aware of the tree outside this hut. It's a way off, but I feel it. Feel its light. Feel the life that pulses in its veins and the rot that encroaches on it slowly, threatening its existence.

The tree calls to me, though. It calls and I answer, reaching out to it. The power that flows through it is mine, if I want it. In some way that I don't understand, I'm connected to the tree. I claim the power, accepting it. As I do, the life-beat of the tree slows.

Caill and I are bigger than the hut. In some strange way, we're both inside of its containment and outside at the same time. Clouds roil in the sky above us. Deep gray, wintry ones clashing against the black clouds of a raging storm. Lightning flashes, bolts streaking across the sky and colliding with each other. As they hit, thunderous booms blast the land below.

People scream but the sound of their terror is distant. Caill dominates the space in front of me but in my head, I see Duncan. I see him die, over and over. The loop is stuck on repeat and every single time my heart shatters. Every time I watch him hit by the bullet and see that spray of blood, the pain is as new and as fresh and as deep. It tears me apart, shredding my insides with claws as sharp as razors.

Caill and I glare at each other and in our glares is the raging storm. I don't know what I'm doing or how. All I care about is saving Duncan. How do I do it? There must be a way.

You ask the wrong question, Dugald's voice says in the back of my head.

A white flash and something like a bolt of lightning hits me in the face. I stumble back to the sound of Caill laughing. I wave a hand and black energy coalesces around my fist, flying free to strike at Caill.

The wrong question. What is the right one?

Caill and I struggle, but the fight isn't with her. It's internal. I'm fighting myself.

The right question.

Power crackles over my skin and then I know. I know the right question.

Why him?

I know why. Now. I would never admit it even to myself before but here, in this moment and in this place the truth is as raw and unavoidable as the rising of the sun. I'm not falling for him. I've fallen.

"I love him," I say it out loud.

Caill closes her eyes, inhales deeply, then lets it out in a long, heavy sigh. The power of our dueling storms sizzles but they lessen.

"Aye, lass."

We glare at each other as raindrops fall around me and huge snowflakes swirl around her. Neither of us are ready or willing to retreat but we're at an impasse. I look past her and see the folks of the village cowering. They hide in their huts, under tables, some on their knees with hands covering their heads.

The glamour of the place is gone. The huts, which were awkwardly, haphazardly cute, aren't. They're afflicted with rot. There are holes in them that weren't there before. Weeds grow along the paths. The people aren't beautiful; they're haggard. Even Caill, who looked old and rather like a fairy tale witch, is worse in my new sight. She's so thin she looks like it's an effort of will alone that keeps her here.

And the tree.

The tree isn't bright and silvery. It's dim, barely lighting, with leaves that have fallen all around it. What leaves it does have are wilted and curled. Black veins run through its trunk and out its limbs. That same blackness that pulses and waits outside the ring of its light. The black void of nothingness. Hopelessness.

"I don't understand," I say, looking around with dawning horror.

The darkness that waits outside the tree's light is alive. It pulsates as finger-like protrusions probe and test the strength of the tree's light, seeking any opening. Some of those dark tendrils reach towards me.

"You can't save him. The past can't be changed," Caill says. There's an intense sadness in her voice.

I shake my head, rejecting her truth. The pain in my chest is so intense it feels as if my heart is rebelling. Pressure builds in my forehead as tears swell behind my eyes.

"Then what is the point? There must be a way."

I reject the sadness even as I reject her statement. No, it can't be. I reach for something and find anger. Then anger burns into rage. A surging, molten force that sears through my veins.

The dark tendrils reach out and touch my foot and in them is power. Power I pull on. As I do, I grow still bigger. I look down on the fae from above, towering over even Caill.

"Quinn, stop!" Caill yells. "Don't do that. You don't know what you're doing."

"I can save him. I know it," I say.

I'm certain that if I pull enough of this power in, I can do anything. The darkness sings as I accept its power, a siren's song in my head. As it flows in, the image of Duncan dying changes. It's so clear. I see exactly how it will happen. I will arrive before he is shot and with a wave of my hands the weapons of the Colquhouns melt. They'll turn and run-in fear but I don't have to let them go. I have no mercy for those who would harm what is mine. Mercy is not required of me for I am power.

"Enough!" a deep voice booms and something cracks.

The power filling me drains away like the gates of a dam have been opened. I shrink to normal size, breathing heavily. Dugald stands next to Caill, glaring. He leans on a thick staff that he twists his hands around.

"What are you thinking?" he barks. "You can't change history. What is, is what is."

"No," I snap. "You're wrong. I felt it. I could do it."

"You would destroy everything," Caill says.

"You can't know that."

I'm arguing with them, but I don't even know why. I can prove them wrong, then they'll see how right I am. I've tasted real power and if nothing else was clear, I know this for sure. I can be more powerful than they are and with that power I can save Duncan.

Dugald and I glare at one another. I try to reach for the power I only just had but I can't. There's a barrier between it and me. Scowling, I try again but something is blocking me. Dugald's forehead crinkles in concentration and then I realize it's him. He's keeping me from saving Duncan.

"Stop it," I demand.

Dugald shakes his head. "You're not ready. You're like a child with a loaded gun."

"I'm not a child," I say. I open my mouth to say more but before I speak, a cat meows.

Something about the incongruousness of a cat interrupting shuts me up. I look down and the biggest cat I've ever seen is looking back at me. It's at least the size of a full-grown German Shepherd with pitch black fur except for a single white patch on its breast. The cat has emerald eyes that reflect the soft light of the tree. It stalks closer until it rubs against my legs purring.

"The Queen will see you now," someone says.

When I look up, there's a brown man there. He's brown everywhere. Brown skin the color of an oak tree's bark with hints of ash gray tones. His haphazard clothes are mismatched browns. Even his long hair that reaches to the middle of his back is brown and ratty.

"Radagast?" I ask, wondering if Tolkien got his inspiration for the character from this fae.

He frowns, wrinkling the rough bark of his face, and shakes his head.

"Come."

I exchange looks with Caill and Dugald both of whom have their heads bowed. Neither of them speak up. The deference in their posture is clear. These two are powerful beings. If they're this quiet, then what am I about to face?

"The Queen, huh? Well, let's do this."

Fear trails ice through my veins as I follow the Brown Man, potentially to my death.

Chapter Twenty-Seven

MY PALMS SWEAT and I breathe raggedly as I follow the Brown Man through the village. My blood pressure creates a dull thudding in my ears as we walk. All the people have resumed their activities as if nothing out of the ordinary has happened. Who knows, maybe all of what I did is normal for them.

We walk in silence, leaving me too much time to think. I don't want to die. I don't know why I think I might, but it feels like it though. I can't die now, not without understanding who I am or what's happening here. Nothing makes sense and the worst part is, I don't recognize myself.

In some way, I feel like I'm more me. As if all the life I lived before coming to the MacGregors was a lie. A waking dream, some kind of half-life. Even here, in these Fae realms, I'm not as weirded out as I rightfully should be. I'm not surprised. On some level I belong here.

But the rational part of me is lost. The rational is at war with the irrational. None of this is possible, but I'm here. I'm experiencing these things. It's happening, like it or not, so where does that leave me?

The Brown Man stops at the base of the tree and waits for me to catch up. I can't not see the mars in the tree bark now that I've glimpsed past the glamours. They look like gashes, each one a knife wound oozing black sap. Revulsion at the wrongness of it clenches my stomach and bile rises in my throat.

"Ready?" the Brown Man asks.

"For?" I ask.

He smiles and even his teeth are a shade of brown. They look like they're carved out of wood, like the rest of him. He holds out his hand. I'm tentative but having come this far, I take it. He jerks me towards him. I stumble forward, yelping, but we're somewhere else. I stumble past him, but he keeps his grip on my arm which stops me from falling.

We're in a room made of stars. It's like we're standing on the night sky itself. The tree is still here, but in reverse. Here it glows darkly, casting a warm blue light instead of silvery. Stars swirl around us, forming and breaking constellations as fast as I look. Milky clouds of dust drift along what must be walls but they don't look like walls. It looks like it goes on forever.

"Welcome, Quinn," a female voice says. The voice is rich and warm; it's a thousand layered voices speaking as one.

I look at the source, but I can only meet her gaze for a moment before looking down and away. She's too... beautiful? Too much? Too there?

To say the Fae Queen is beautiful is far too inadequate. She *is* beauty. Austere, yet warm, her skin the color of pure white milk and her hair the frosty, pure, untouched snow of a mountain top. Her eyes remind me of Duncan's, ice blue and piercing. The one moment I met those eyes, she knew me through and through.

I make an awkward attempt at a curtsy.

"Your Majesty," I say.

"Come, child," she says, gesturing with her fingers for me to come closer.

My heart thunders in my ears. My mouth is dry and my head hurts from building pressure, but I walk forward. I still can't look directly at her, keeping her in my peripheral vision while focusing most of my attention on the floor which is disconcerting enough since I'm walking on stars. Still, it's easier than meeting her eyes.

When I'm about an arm's length from her, I stop. I swallow hard and focus my thoughts. If anyone can help save Duncan, it's going to be her. That's what matters.

"I need to get back," I say. "I have to save Duncan."

"Do you?"

"Yes," I say, biting off the harsh feelings that come with her question. "I do."

"I see."

I wait for more, but she doesn't speak. The stars spiral across the night sky view as I wait in uncomfortable silence.

"And?" she asks.

"And what?"

"I need to go back. I must save the MacGregors," I say, because maybe if it's the entire clan she'll help but the truth burns in my chest and falls off my tongue unbidden. "I have to save him."

"You can't."

It's such a simple statement but a knife thrust into my chest couldn't hurt any more than it does. Anger surges and I meet her eyes full on, using the anger to reaffirm my resolve.

"Then what is the point? What's the point of any of this?" I throw my arms up in exasperation. "Why me? Why was I put there? Why am I here?"

"You are our last hope. You are the Destroyer."

"And what the devil does that mean? I'm not special. I'm... a girl. A nobody."

"Are you?"

"Of course I am. What else would I be?"

"So, a 'girl', as you say it, isn't important? A 'nobody' has no impact? Is not capable?"

"That's not what I said."

"Isn't it?" She frowns and the room around us dims, as if night is somehow darker than it was, the stars further away.

"No, well, yes, but that's not what I'm talking about. I'm talking about me."

"Every choice matters." She shrugs. "Some people's choices matter more than others."

"What does that mean?"

The Queen smiles and the stars pulse brighter.

"You are so full of questions," the Queen says. "Come, break your fast with me."

She motions with one arm and a table laden with food appears out of nowhere. The smells are incredible. There are roasted meats that glisten with spice and juices; succulent sweets that make my mouth water with their scent; pitchers full of mulled wine; and bread so fresh and fluffy looking I want to hold it in my hands to experience it.

I stare at the table and something niggles at the back of my mind. Something Alesoun said. A warning... What was it?

And if'n ya eat the food of the fae, you're bound to them, same as blood.

"No, thank you, I'm not hungry," I lie.

The Fae Queen only smiles, but it's a knowing smile. As if she knows the lie, seeing it fall from my lips. I can't let her distract me like this. I have to get back and when I do, I need to get back with power. Power like I felt facing down Caill. With that power I can save the MacGregor clan. I can save Duncan.

"As you wish," she says, taking a glass of wine and swirling it in her hand. She watches me over the gold rim of the glass.

"How do I get back?"

"To?"

"The MacGregors, of course."

"Not your own time?"

That stops the flood of words in my head. My own time. My

friends, school, and my Dad. Leaving the MacGregors to their fate, a fate that everyone I've met here says can't be changed.

My lips tingle with the memory of Duncan's kiss. His arms around me, the feel of my breasts crushing against his strong chest. The scent of him fills my nostrils, overwhelming even the succulent scents of the offered food.

"No," I say, making a decision I didn't know I was going to have to make. "I don't know how. I don't know why, but I know Duncan. I've known him. We're connected, and I must save him."

"And?"

"Huh? And? And what?"

"Exactly."

"He doesn't deserve to die."

"He's a thief. He's killed men. By what judgment does he not deserve his fate?"

"He's not a thief. Or a killer. He's doing what he has to do to survive."

"And that end justifies the means? What places his survival above those of the men he's killed? Those whose survival he's endangered by stealing their own livelihood. Is it because he's stronger?"

"No. I don't know." I shake my head, not caring about her disagreements. "You're muddying the point. He's a good man."

The Queen watches me, waiting with an unreadable look on her face. I put my hands on my hips and meet her gaze.

"He doesn't deserve to die. None of them do, not like what is coming."

"And what is it that is coming?"

"Their very name will be outlawed. They'll be hunted, like animals. Forced to fight in pits. They'll kill them. Man, woman, child, they'll kill them all."

"Not so different," she says.

"What do you mean?"

She shakes her head. "Now is not the time. You cannot change the past. What is, is what will be."

"Then what is the point?" I ask, frustration rising. "Why bother bringing me to that place? Why did I meet him? Why did I meet any of them?"

"The past *is* but that doesn't mean you are not."

"That makes no sense."

"If the past is as it was, then your presence there is what was."

My mouth drops open as the implications of what she's saying hits me.

"You mean I'm supposed to be there. Whatever I do is what was supposed to happen."

"Mostly, yes."

"Then you can send me back to them. That means I can save them."

"No."

"No? But you just said—"

She holds up one finger stopping me.

"I said what was supposed to happen is what will happen. You cannot save all the MacGregors. Their fate is sealed. That does not mean you cannot help. That you cannot, perhaps, save the one you care so much for."

"And the rest?"

She shakes her head. My heart flutters in my chest as I consider her words.

"Okay, I want to save him."

"Good. Drink this."

I stare at the offered cup. Her long, snowy-white fingers are wrapped delicately around it, holding it out as the most natural thing in the world. Except it's not. It's a binding, a contract, that places a hold over me in some way I don't fully understand.

"What is it you're asking of me?"

"That you accept your role. Take on your destiny, before it overtakes you."

"I don't know what my destiny is. How do I embrace it?"

"Listen to your heart. It will tell you."

"Nice. Cryptic. Vague. Love it. Are the stories true? If I eat or drink Fae food, am I bound to your realm?"

Her smile doesn't leave her face, but it does fade from her eyes. She pulls the drink away and turns her back on me.

"Yes," she says. She turns back around, and her perfect skin has signs of age on it now. Her hair is no longer lush, but lank. She looks dimmer, somehow less. "And no."

"What is happening here?" I ask, sweeping one arm wide to take in all the Fae realms.

"Have they not told you? We are dying. As your world progresses, our world is fading away."

"And what is it I'm supposed to do about it?"

"You are the Destroyer. We cannot make that change for you. We can only play our role in your story."

"My story?" I ask, numbness creeping along my limbs.

She nods. The cold numbing sensation invades my chest, stretching towards my heart, making it hard to breathe.

I drop onto a bench by the table. "Why me?"

"Tell me of your mother," the Queen says.

"I didn't know her well, she died when I was very young. I was raised by my Dad."

"What do you remember of your mother?"

"Her smile," I say, the image coming unbidden: Mother smiling as she looks down on me in my crib.

"What else?"

"What else? She told me stories of Scotland. I remember her rocking me while regaling me with tales of the beauty of it. Sometimes she'd tell me about the Fae. It doesn't matter, she was there, then she was gone." The bitterness that I keep locked away in the deepest corners of my mind tries to break free, but I push it back down. "Whatever. She has nothing to do with anything."

"If that was true, then you would not be lashing out with such anger."

"I'm not angry," I yell and rise to my feet. "Not about her at least. I'm angry about this. This place. This situation. You. All I want is a chance to explore these feelings with Duncan. I—"

"You what?"

My mouth moves but the word won't come. It's so hard to admit it. I love him. I can't, by any logic in the universe, love him, but I do. The way he makes me feel like I'm special. The way he looks at me, even when he's being a stubborn ass and not listening.

"I think I love him."

The Queen nods then she laughs which sounds like sleigh bells bouncing across a winter field.

"The choice is yours, Destroyer," she says, wiping a glistening tear from her eye. "As it always is. As it always will be. You can go back, you can try to save him, but to do so you must drink."

Watching her as she nonchalantly waves at the spread of food and treats, I replay the conversation in my head. Something about it sticks in my mind.

"Why did you ask about my mother?"

"You need to make your choice."

She motions at the table once again but now I notice she's the one not meeting my eyes. She's avoiding the question.

"No, wait. You asked about my mother. Why? What do you know about her?"

She places one delicate, impossibly white finger over her rosy lips and makes a shh sound.

"Hush, child. Even here, the darkness is listening."

Chills crawl down my spine and I look around, trying to identify the creeping sensation but there's nothing visible. Still, I can't shake the feeling that we're being watched now that she has called attention to it.

"What do you mean?"

She only smiles in answer.

"You can save him," she says. "Maybe, but your opportunity is slipping away."

"If I eat or drink, the story says I'll be bound to the Fae realm. Is it true?"

"Are you not already bound to us?"

"Can you not ever answer a simple question? Is everything a question back?" I move closer to her until I'm right up in her face. "I can't make a decision without knowing the truth."

"Truth is simplicity. A simplicity you are not ready for."

"Cryptic. Great. Does it tie me to you?"

She smiles and nods. "You are already bound to us but yes, it will strengthen your ties to the fae."

"Then what?"

"You are the Destroyer, Quinn. The choice is, and always will be, yours."

"And if I do this, can I save him?"

"I did not say that."

"You said maybe and that my opportunity is slipping away."

She sighs. "Here is a truth for you. I cannot lie. I will not. Ever. What I tell you is the truth, to the best of my knowledge."

"But you never answer a question."

She smiles ruefully and gestures at the table. "Eat. Or drink. Then go."

Uncertainty swamps my thoughts like a river breaking its banks then surging through town and carrying refuse and debris along with it. Random thoughts, pieces of memory, dance through my head. I can sit here and do nothing, or I can do *something*.

When in doubt, act. Dad used to say that. Or close enough. I grab the glass the Queen had previously offered. It's an ornate gold goblet encrusted with gems. I stare at it for a long moment, listening to my heartbeat. This drink is going to bind me to the fae, but if there is even a chance I can save Duncan, then I have to take it.

Taking a deep breath, I drain the goblet.

The last thing I see is the Fae Queen smile as the world fades to white.

Chapter Twenty-Eight

I STUMBLE THEN DROP onto my hands and knees in thick, highland grass. My stomach clenches. I retch then vomit as my insides rebel against whatever the hell just happened. I wipe my mouth on my sleeve and, shakily, I climb to my feet.

"Thanks," I mutter. "Nice trip."

My tongue tingles from the spiced, mulled wine. It's not unpleasant but a bit odd that the taste of it is still lingering. My taste buds scream with desire for more, but I guess they'll have to get over it. I force myself to keep standing despite my shaky legs and trembling arms. My belly tries to rebel again, but I press my hands against it and manage not to give in to the nausea.

I blink, forcing my eyes to adjust to the dark. The spiraling stars are bright, and the partial moon gives enough light. I turn in a circle until I see the standing stone that I followed Dugald to.

"Good, I know where I'm at. This is good." I wipe sweat from my forehead with my forearm and take a deep breath of the cool night air. "Right. Get up. Quit wasting time. Back to the village."

Chewing my cheek, I turn around to head to the village. The dark seems menacing in ways it hasn't before, as if it's no longer only an absence of light but a thing. A consciousness that's waiting. I feel its anticipation. Infinitely patient and prepared to pounce. I shiver, close my eyes, and take a deep breath, but when I open them, the feeling is still there.

"Quinn!" Duncan's voice is faint and distant.

"Duncan," I shout and run towards the sound of his voice.

"Quinn? Is it you?"

"Duncan. Here!"

We shout back and forth until he climbs over a ridge. My heart leaps into my throat and tears swell in my eyes. The sight of him is a punch to the guts and I can't catch my breath. The moonlight illuminates him in soft silvery light. He stands tall and strong, broad shoulders, square jaw, and his long hair blowing in a gentle breeze. He's a striking figure in any light, but this is too posed, too perfect.

"Quinn," he yells. It breaks the instant of perfection as he bursts into a flat out run towards me.

His sword slaps against his back as he bounds across the distance. I don't wait, sprinting towards him. In a small part of my head, I recognize this as some cheesy romance movie moment. The two lovers run into each other's arms, but I don't care. I'm so happy to see him and know that he's still alive.

We crash into each other, and he takes the force of our collision by using it to lift me off my feet. He spins me around, holding me up against the night sky, then he crushes me against himself. I find his lips and claim the first kiss.

His heady, musky scent fills my nose. His lips are warm and full as they press onto mine. I drive my tongue into his mouth and twine my fingers in his glorious hair. My grasping, clutching, and kissing are tinged with desperation and fear. Fear of having lost him. Having seen him die over and over. But he is here. We're here, together, now. We have this moment and I have this one chance to save him.

"Quinn," he gasps, pulling back and breaking the kiss. "Are ya alright?"

"Aye." I laugh and jerk his head closer to kiss him again.

He lowers me to my feet and I wrap one arm around his neck, pressing into him. My breasts rub against the rough cloth of my blouse crushing against him. Desire is a raging inferno in my lower belly. I want him.

No, I need him.

I run my hand over his shoulder and down his arm, feeling the strength in his biceps and triceps, then trailing back up to come down across his muscled chest. His shirt is thick but there's no hiding those muscles or the hard body beneath it.

He gives into the intensity of my kiss, running his hands through my hair and down my back, and then groping my ass. His tongue meets mine, moving with it, accepting me into him. His cock hardens, digging into my lower belly, and I keep my free hand moving down, intent on having it.

As I slide my hand under his kilt, I'm pleased to find the old myths are true about what a Scotsman wears beneath it. I grab his hard member and squeeze. He groans into our kiss, and he shifts his hips so he's thrusting himself into my hand.

Our mouths become inseparable as I work my hand down his shaft to find his balls. I gently squeeze them, rolling them in my hand then stroking my fingers across them and back up to grab his shaft.

"Quinn," he gasps, breaking the kiss. "Are ya sure? We do nae have to."

"Hush," I say, placing my hand over his mouth.

He sucks my fingers, and it feels like I'm gushing in my nether regions. My mouth fills with saliva and I know what I want to do. What I need. He grabs my wrist then takes my fingers, one at a time and sucks them in his mouth. As he does, I lower myself to my knees and lift his kilt.

His hard member is erect and ready. Without hesitating, I take the head into my mouth and hold it, swirling my tongue around the hard ridge of the glans. He gasps and thrusts his hips forward. I let him slide in deeper, keeping my mouth wide. Once he stops his forward thrust, I work my tongue around the shaft while sucking.

He groans and I do too. He kisses my fingers, strokes my face and hair. No guy I've ever been with has ever given me attention like this and it feels amazing. I slide up and down his shaft, working him deeper into my throat. I use my free hand to tug on his balls, pulling them gently down then squeezing, releasing, and repeating the motion.

When his dick swells in my mouth and he stops working my fingers to gasp air, I know he's about to lose it. I grab his balls and squeeze, not too hard but hard enough to distract him from losing his load. It works perfectly.

I pull my mouth off his cock and rise to my feet. He kisses me without hesitation, which makes me love him all the more. Wrapping his arms around my waist, he lowers me to the ground as we work together to get my dress up past my waist.

I leave the skirt to him in favor of freeing my breasts. I undo the tie of my blouse until it's loose enough that they are exposed to the night air. My nipples are dark and hard, flushed with blood from all the attention, cool air, and pent-up desire.

Hovering over me outlined by the gentle light of the moon, Duncan stops and stares. He has his mouth open, and his eyes are alight with desire staring at my exposed breasts. His mouth moves as if he's going to speak but no sound comes. It's no more than a heartbeat but it's one of those moments that freezes in time. Instead of speaking, he drops his head, taking one nipple in his mouth.

His rough tongue lashes my hard nipple. I gasp in surprise; my nipples have always been extremely sensitive. Pleasure mixes with a hint of pain. He sucks on my tit while his tongue rolls around the nipple. I buck my hips against him as his attention makes my pussy wetter.

He breaks his suction seal on my breast and slides up between my legs, one hand between us as he guides his cock home. He stares into my eyes as the head of his dick presses against my opening.

I bite my lower lip, my eyes half-closed. The stars array to outline him, the galactic dust of the Milky Way stretching across the night sky. Then he thrusts. I'm ready, so, so ready. He slides in, fully seating himself in me, and holds.

We both gasp. I wrap my fingers in his hair, tilting my head back and groaning softly. He feels so good. His cock fills the aching empty need. His chest rests on mine, and I feel his heart as if it's the thundering hoofbeats of a stampede. My own heart responds, coming into time with him.

Slowly, in an impressive display of control and will, he slides out. Emptiness flows behind his exit and I groan at the loss, but it is momentary. He slides back in and as he does, he lowers his lips to mine.

We kiss as we commit our bodies to each other. The ultimate affirmation of life. In the face of his death that I know is coming, I give myself to him. Or I take him. I take him to be mine, into not only my bed or my arms, but into my heart.

I'm going to save him. He will live. If I am what they claim, if I am the Destroyer, then I will destroy any who try to harm him.

Our bodies find the natural rhythm that comes as two people learn from each other. Hips moving in time with beating hearts. Speeding up as we build towards the ultimate climax. I feel it coming, building in the same way I can feel a thunderstorm building. It gently grows like the storm clouds gathering.

Disaster sits right over the horizon and none of us are ready but right now, at this moment, I am staking my claim. Duncan is mine and I am his. I will do whatever it takes to save him.

He thrusts and twists his hips in a way that is so pleasing it is as if this is our hundredth time together, not our first. He knows what I like, how I like it, and what will push me to the finite yet infinite edge that I dance on before the orgasm takes over.

We hang together, each thrust harder, deeper, driving towards the cliff. I dig my nails into his back as we teeter together then as one, we fall. My pleasure is blinding in its intensity. There is no other thought, no other world beyond the two of us.

"Quinn," he gasps, shuddering as aftershocks rush through him and his dick spasms deep inside of me.

Miniature orgasms continue through my body as we hold each other and kiss until at last his dick softens and he pulls out. He rolls over and lies beside me. I shift, putting my head on his shoulder, and listen to his breath and heart.

We lie underneath the moon and stars while the earth spins on, and I think of nothing as long as I can. But I can hold my problems at bay for only so long. They come crashing back and bring the harshness of reality with them.

Somehow, I have to stop what I know is coming. I must change history, no matter what the Fae says is impossible. If I can't, if the MacGregors go for retribution on the Colquhouns, the wheels of history will crush them.

I don't want this moment to end. I love lying here, staring at the wide-open sky. Counting stars as he idly plays with my hair with one hand and his other traces small circles across my body. But want and reality are at war and in this case, with these stakes, reality wins.

"What day is tomorrow?" I ask.

"Tomorrow? Does it matter?"

"How long until the clan is going to seek retribution? What day is it?"

"Ach, it is the sixth of February, Year of Our Lord 1603," he says after a moment's thought.

"Shit."

He raises himself onto an elbow and rests his head on his hand while looking at me. "What's wrong?" I remember now. The seventh is when the MacGregors fight the Colquhouns and they'll win. They'll do more than win. It's a massacre, which is all the justification the Colquhouns and their secret allies the Campbells and the Bruces need to get the King of England to outlaw the MacGregor name.

Dawning horror rushes through me; bile rises in my throat. This is it. My last chance to save him, to save them.

Chapter Twenty-Nine

MY HEART THUNDERS in my chest as I sit up and twist to look directly at Duncan. He rises to a sitting position, taking my hands in his. I swallow down the bile and focus my thoughts. I have one chance, but I have to make him believe me.

"Duncan, I need you to listen to me."

"Ach, lass, I'm sorry for what I said before," he says. "I was a fool. I know you're nae a witch and if'n ya are, I do nae care. Mother Mary bless me, I don't."

"Sorry? No, that? That's nothing. You have nothing to be sorry for, it doesn't matter. Listen," I say.

"No, you're nae right. I am sorry. I should nae have given in to my urges."

"Duncan, what are you talking about?"

"What I did to ya. It was nae right. I should nae have taken such advantage of ya."

He stands up and seems unable to meet my eyes. He straightens his clothes and looks anywhere but me. He offers me his hand, still avoiding eye contact. I straighten my shirt, putting my girls away, and pull my skirt back down while staring at him in disbelief.

"Duncan—"

"Ach, I know," he interrupts me. "You do nae have to admonish me. It was wrong of me. I cannae apologize enough."

"Duncan—"

"Quin, I do nae know what overcame me. The Devil moved in my thoughts." He's talking a mile a minute. His held-out hand trembles. "I will go to see tha priest. I'll do confession. Tell me how I can make it up to ya—"

"Duncan."

"Anything ya want, I'll—"

I climb to my feet without taking his hand. He is half-turned away from me, still trying to avoid my gaze. Even in the soft moonlight, I can see the flush on his face. I grab his shoulder and pull but he resists my gentle effort to turn him around.

"Please, lemme help ya back to tha village, to Alesoun's place. I promise you'll be safe in my company."

"Duncan, damn it." I jerk on his shoulder with all my strength.

It's enough to force him to turn towards me though he keeps his eyes downcast. I cup his chin, the rough of his beard prickly against the palm of my hand as I pull up. At long last, his eyes meet mine.

"Quinn—"

"Shut. Up." I rise onto my toes.

I kiss him and the passion rushes back like a tidal wave. I only intended to give him a brief, reassuring kiss, but his lips on mine stir latent desires and feelings, none of which are yet satisfied despite our amazing encounter. I can't get enough of him and judging by the way he gives himself into the kiss, he feels the same.

When my lungs are burning to the point I can't not take a breath, I break the kiss. He bows his feverish forehead onto mine and we lean on each other, panting until our hearts slow and breathing returns to something closer to normal.

"I am sorry, lass. I cannae seem to control myself with ya."

"Fine," I answer, half-laughing. "I get it. Truthfully, I can't either, but listen. You don't have anything to be sorry for. I wanted this as much as you did. Is that a sin? If it is, then let us be sinners."

"Quinn, no! You cannae mean that."

"Duncan, please, shut up." I have such a small window to convince him of the truth of what's coming I can't waste it on talk of us or sex or worry about his offended values. "There are more important things to talk about right now, ones that can't wait."

"But our souls," he protests.

"Good lord, man. I get it. I appreciate it, but can we put a pin in it?"

"Put a what in it? I do nae understand."

I admonish myself for using idioms that probably won't be invented for another hundred years or whatever.

"It doesn't matter," I say, waving it away with my hand. "Listen, we can talk about ourselves and what happened later, okay?"

"But—"

I place my hand over his mouth.

"No. No *buts*. Not now, got it?"

He nods.

"Good." I chew my lower lip. How do I do this? Knowing I have to get him to understand and having an actual plan to do that aren't coming together. "You believe in the Fair folk, right?"

"Aye, of course I do."

"Okay, good."

He already thinks I might be a witch and at this point, going full in on his belief and superstition may be the only way to make sure he doesn't end up dead. I can only hope saving his life doesn't cost me having him for myself but if that's the price, I'll pay it.

"But what of it? You cannae be having affairs with them. It's dangerous. All the tales say so, and it might even be an affront to God."

"It's not," I say without thought. I have no idea if it does or doesn't offend God, but I reject the idea on principle alone. After all, if God made everything, then he made the Fae too. "But that's not what matters. I've been to the Fae realms."

"No," Duncan says, eyes widening. He grabs me and roughly runs his hands up and down my arms, over my face, feeling me as if he's making sure I'm really here. "Are ya alright? How did ya get home? What happened?"

"I'm fine. Really, stop," I say, grabbing his arms and forcing him to quit pawing at me like I'm some kind of animal. The rejection on his face fills me with regret but there's no time for this. "I'm sorry. Listen, we don't have much time."

"Time for what?"

"To save you," I say. "To save your entire clan."

"My clan? What do ya mean?"

"I tried to tell you," I say. "You cannot go to battle. You have to stop the clan from going after the Colquhouns. The King of England is looking for an excuse, any excuse, to bring hell down on the MacGregors."

His face shifts from rejection to cold hard steel. Steel that glints in his eyes, forms the hard line of his clenched jaw, and appears in the corded muscles of his arms.

"If that English bastard wants a fight, then he can come and we'll give him more than he ever imagined."

"Duncan, you can't."

"I can. We can. You do nae know the MacGregors if'n you think we'll back down from a fight."

"It's not a fight, Duncan. It's not even a war. It's going to be a massacre."

"Aye, it will be," he agrees grimly. "English blood will water the Highlands."

"No." Frustration fills my chest and tears swell in my eyes. "I mean, sure, it will, but not enough. The MacGregors will come out the worse for it. They'll hunt you down, like animals, chasing you off into the Highlands. They'll kill any MacGregor on sight."

"That will nae happen," he says. "You do nae know my clan.

We'll fight them and we'll win. They cannae stand against us. They come for the MacGregors and the other clans will rise up with us."

"They can. They will. Listen to me, please." I'm pleading but he's not listening. The lust for battle burns on his face as clear as if it's the sun in the sky. "You have to believe me."

"Believe what, lass? That you do nae think myself and my clan can fight a war? That we'd rather run from a fight than to face it?"

"No, that's not it. Damn it, Duncan. Listen."

"Bah, I am sorry for my mistreatment of ya, but that doesn't mean I'm going to drop my balls and run from a fight. What kind of man would I be for ya then? You're too fine a woman to have a coward for a husband."

A husband? Too fine? Oh, my god. Is he thinking that far ahead? Is he proposing?

I grit my teeth and push that aside. It won't matter in the slightest if I don't change the future. Unbidden and unwanted, the memory of seeing him die plays in my mind's eye, smashing the happier thoughts.

"It's not about being a coward," I shout. "I told you, I went to the fae lands."

"And what of it? Did they magically show you the future? Did they give you some strange vision or sight that lets you know what you cannae possibly—"

"Yes!"

He stops mid-sentence, his mouth hanging slack.

"Yes, I did. I have seen the future and it's bad. So bad I don't care if you call me a witch. I don't care because, damn it, I can't lose you. I care too much about you. I don't want you or any of the clan to die."

He stares as my heart thumps like a rabbit. It's beating so fast, I can't count the number of beats. Anticipation makes my skin crawl, the hairs on my arms stand on end, and the back of my neck itches. I want him to speak. I need him to say something.

Anything. At long last, he opens his mouth and I swear it's in slow motion.

"You care about me?" he asks, breaking the silence.

"Of course I do, you big oaf," I say with a sob.

I can't hold back the tears that burst forth, trailing hot streaks down my cheeks. I rub the rough stubble of his beard and trace the line of his jaw.

"Ya care about me..." he mutters, trailing off.

Then he grabs me with strong arms and crushes me into his embrace. His mouth smashes onto mine with bruising force and our teeth click together but the pain is inconsequential. The pent-up emotions and fears uncork, exploding out like a shaken champagne bottle.

He kisses me with an intensity and a passion that I've never felt in my life. It feels different than any kiss I've known. Different than even those we've already shared. It's not only physical, so much more than our lips simply moving together. The us that is more than our bodies are moving together. As if we're coming into a wonderful synchronicity.

It's a claim too. Animalistic. Primal. A kiss that is marking what he claims as his but that goes both ways. I'm also claiming him. He's mine. I'm choosing him and I know, in my heart of hearts, that this is what is supposed to be.

This is why it feels like I've known him longer than I have. In some way, we're shedding skins, revealing truths that I don't fully comprehend. I know, on some deep level, that this is what must be. What has always been and what will always be.

He breaks the kiss and we hold each other, staring into one another's eyes with unbridled wonder. Understanding each other in new ways and yet still seeing more mysteries in each other to be explored. He trails the fingers of one hand across my cheek and I turn into his touch, kissing his palm.

"Tell me," he says at last. "Tell me everything."

I do. Or the best I can of it. I hold back the power I gathered while facing Caill because I don't understand it myself. I don't think I could put it into words if I tried and if I managed, it'd clearly mark me as a witch. Right now, I'm as much a victim as the protagonist which suits the situation fine. He asks questions as I relay the story, pulling out odd things to put attention on but I answer them all to the best of my ability until at last I've told him all of it.

"And you're nae telling tales?" he asks at last.

"No," I say, shaking my head.

"You're really from the future?"

"I am."

He shakes his head. "And you came here to... what?"

"I don't know."

He inhales deeply then lets it out in a long, heavy sigh.

"Well," he says, "we have our work cut out for us, do we nae?"

"Our work?"

"Aye," he says. "We need to figure out why you're here."

"We need to stop your clan from going to war."

"Tha' will nae be easy," he says. "They're on the way to fight as we speak."

I grab his shoulders and grip them tight.

"Duncan, we have to stop them. If we don't..." I swallow hard. "It's bad."

"I hear ya," he says. "All we can do is try."

The first rays of the sunrise stretch across the highlands. I take a deep breath, inhaling the fresh, cold Scottish air. The scent of peat and heather are heavy and fill my head, clearing my thoughts.

"There is no try," I say with my eyes closed. I open them and meet his icy-blue ones. "It's do or do not. And we must do. No matter how dangerous it is."

Chapter Thirty

"THEY'VE QUITE THE LEAD," Duncan says, holding out his hand. I take his hand as he points past the standing stone, away from the village. "If we run, we might be able to cut across the Highlands and intercept them."

"We have to try," I say.

Running in full length, layered skirts with rough leather shoes is a lot harder than I would have ever given it credit. Any girl who manages it has my admiration. We don't get far before I'm breathing heavily, stumbling to a stop.

"Maybe you should run ahead," I huff.

"This is nae our territory. I cannae leave you here alone."

Gasping to try and catch my breath with hands on knees, I look around. "We're still in the highlands."

"Aye, but once we went past that standing stone, we entered into lands claimed by Clan Bruce."

"Ah. Okay," I say, straightening. I heave in a deep breath and nod. "I'll try."

I push myself towards a run but the best I manage is a jog. The ground is uneven, and the thick grass randomly gives way to soft peat. When I step on a patch, my foot sinks in and I stumble.

When we hit patches of heather, they're the worst to get through. Duncan avoids them whenever possible, cutting around them even if it is off our intended path.

"You're doin' fine," he says, never letting go of my hand.

"Liar," I say, coming to a halt again.

The sun is not quite up to midday, but I'm exhausted. Duncan offers me his water skin which I accept gratefully. The stale water is like the finest cup of fresh ground coffee. I'm so thirsty I gulp it down.

"Ach, we've not made bad time."

"But not good enough, right?" I ask, wiping sweat off my brow and shoving the cork back into his water skin. I hand it back to him as he frowns and shakes his head.

"Probably not."

I take a deep breath then try unsuccessfully to suppress a yawn.

"You need to rest. You'll be better if you do."

"We don't have time," I say. "If we don't stop them from killing the Colquhouns, it's all over."

"I know that's what you saw in the Fae realms," he says. "And I know you're from the future or what have you, but are ya sure? How do ya know ya haven't already changed fate? Also how do ya know ya can trust the Fae?"

"That I don't know," I say. "But I know what the history books say."

"There are books about my people?"

"Yeah," I say, pursing my lips.

I need to keep my mouth shut. What if I tell him too much? What if I say the wrong thing and completely bone history? Change it all? My guts twist into a cold, icy knot. I've been so self-absorbed I hadn't even considered the implications of what I'm doing.

You are the Destroyer. The choice is always yours.

"Sounds amazing," he says. "What else can ya tell me? About the future, where you come from?"

I smile and touch his arm. "It's not grand. Trust me. And I'd best not say more."

"But how do we know?" he asks. "All the tales say the Fae are not to be trusted. At the very least, they're working for their own, unknowable ends. I can trust you, Quinn, but trusting the Fae? That's a wee bit harder to swallow."

"Don't. Don't trust them. Believe me, I don't." Even as I say it, I see him die again, in my head. Again and again, it's running on a loop at the edge of my awareness. I have to wonder if I'm being misled by the Fae? Is it all a lie? Some kind of sick manipulation? I don't know he dies. Are they using my knowledge to push me towards what they want me to do? "We need to keep moving."

"Right," he says, shaking his head. "Fae and girl from the future."

"Yeah," I say as we run.

We don't bother trying to talk. The sun begins its descent towards the horizon and still we run. Dark clouds form on top of the mountains. Streaks of lightning dance across the sky, electric fingers stretching out as Mother Nature prepares to assert her dominance.

When the wind picks up and blows across us, I'm grateful for its cool breath. Exhaustion weighs me down. It feels like I've been carrying a massive pack on my back. Every step, my muscles protest, flashing hot pain as they tremble. My breath burns in and out of my lungs. I'm not sure how long I can keep going.

Duncan seems tireless, an endless well of strength and energy. He doesn't even seem to be breathing heavy, not like I am. He could be out on a stroll across his beautiful homeland. The sky darkens as we run, too early for night fall. The stormfront is overtaking us and there's nothing we can do. I can't run any faster.

"How much further?" I pant.

Duncan looks around before answering. "We're not tha' far. The last I knew, the plan was to find them at Glen Fruin. We're nae far from it now."

Glen Fruin. I remember the name. The MacGregors were outnumbered, almost eight hundred Colquhouns marching into the Highlands while the MacGregors numbered only four hundred. And yet they'll win. They'll win the battle but lose a war they don't even know they're fighting.

"You should run ahead," I say as I stumble to a stop. "I'm past my second, third, and fourth wind. I can't go on."

The stitch in my side won't quit. I can't get a deep enough breath no matter how I try. Duncan touches my face, stooping down so he's looking into my eyes.

"That I cannae do," he says. "I'll nae leave your side, Quinn."

"Duncan, I—"

An enormous cracking sound cuts me off.

Chapter Thirty-One

I JUMP IN SURPRISE, hunching even as I try to look in all directions at once for the source of the terrifying sound. Duncan jerks on my arm and pulls me down into a crouch next to him. He isn't looking around wild-eyed; he's pointing in the direction we were running.

"Stay low," he says, and I barely hear him as the sounds of screaming men reach us followed by more guns firing and the clash of steel on steel.

"We're too late," I say, despair making my voice quaver.

"Aye," he says.

It's done, the Fae Queen said. Caill had also said I was already too late.

They can't be right. This can't be it. I can't give up, not when we're this close.

"Duncan, what if—" I cut myself off as the vision of him running onto the field of battle pushes to the front of my thoughts. What if he wasn't with the original group? What if that happens now? What if it happens next? "We need to leave. We need to run."

"I cannae leave my clan," he says, just as I knew he would.

My heart drops and my stomach clenches. I see it clearly now. The road laid out before me is as real as if I'm standing at a crossroads and the choice is mine. One path leads to his death; the other he will live, but he might hate me after. And as far as I can see down either path, there is no saving the MacGregor Clan. The best I can do is save him. Maybe. Hopefully.

You are the Destroyer. The Fae Queen's voice reverberates through my head.

"Duncan, listen, you have to believe me."

"I've already gone too far to do otherwise, have I nae?"

"Right, I get it, but listen. The MacGregors are going to win."

"You said that we'd be destroyed. That the MacGregors would be outlawed."

"Right, I know what I said," I say. "That happens after this. It happens because of this. We can't stop that. We're too late for that."

"I have to try," he says, rising from his crouch and taking a step forward.

"No." I grab his arm and pull him around to face me.

"Quinn, I will nae stand by and let my clan be slaughtered. You cannae ask that of me."

"I'm not, listen. They win. That's the problem. They're going to slaughter the Colquhouns. Alister is a brilliant tactician. They'll win but they won't just win—they're going to slaughter them."

"Slaughter?"

"Yes, they'll kill so many of them that the King of England will call it a barbarous act. That's how the Colquhouns and the Bruces win. They leverage this slaughter and use it to manipulate the King into outlawing your name so that they can steal your lands."

"I have to stop it!"

"You can't!" I scream. "How do I get you to see it? You can't! It's already happened. They tried to tell me, but I didn't want to listen. Didn't want to believe it, but I see it now. All I can do is save you. It's all the change I can make happen. You can't go to the fight."

"Who tried to tell you? What are you saying?"

"The Fae. They told me that what is written is what is, but I didn't believe them. I didn't want to. I saw you die, Duncan. Over and over, I saw you die and I can't have that. I can't lose you."

"But what can't you change? If you can't change it, if my fate is to die, then I'll meet it with honor. I'm nae a coward, lass."

I shake my head, pulling on his arm as he tries to move away, forcing him to stay. The storm breaks and rain pours down, drenching both of us in moments. I'm grateful for it only because it hides the tears I can't hold back.

"Duncan, no. I can't change all of it, but I can change this. This one thing," I put my hands on his beautiful face and kiss him, but he doesn't respond to my kiss.

"I cannae," he says. "Quinn, I'm sorry but I cannae stand by and let my people be slaughtered. What kind of man would I be if I did that?"

"You're not listening," I say, begging. "They don't die. Not today."

"Then I need to stop them from slaughtering the Colquhouns. If they win but take prisoners, that will change it."

"I don't know that. You don't know that."

Lightning strikes close to hand, blinding us, and thunder reverberates against my chest and leaves my ears ringing.

"Quinn, I have to try."

I stare into his eyes. This is who he is. His core principles, the defining traits that make him who he is. I can't hold him back. I can't change him anymore than I can change the course of history.

"I know," I sob, giving up. "I know. Let's go."

"You should wait here," he says. "I'll come back for ya."

I shake my head, wet hair plastered to my face. I'm a mess but I don't care. I'm going to see this through, no matter the end that is coming.

"I'm with you," I say.

He shakes his head, sending droplets of water spraying off his long hair. He opens his mouth to protest then snaps it shut. Lightning arcs across the sky again, reversing the world as it flashes bright, casting it all into black and white.

Outside the world is bright white light but inside I feel the darkness behind it, just as I did in the lands of the Fae. The darkness is alive and waiting with predatory intent. A shiver races down my spine from much more than the cold rain.

"Fine," he says at last.

He leads the way, holding my hand. The rain slows us down. He picks our way around pools of water and ground too soft to cross as the peat turns swampy. It takes most of my attention to watch my feet and make sure I'm stepping where he does.

A raven caws, its screech cutting through the blowing wind and the pouring rain. I look up. The raven is sitting on top of a standing stone maybe twenty yards away. It seems to be looking past us instead of at me like it usually does.

I cry out in pain, my stomach cramping. The pain is so bad I double over, clasping my arms over my stomach.

"What is it?" Duncan asks, grabbing both of my arms.

"My stomach," I say. "It hurts really bad."

It feels like a fist has clenched my belly tight. Or a miniature blackhole inside is trying to pull all my guts into a hyper compressed ball. It's worse than anything I've ever experienced.

The raven screeches again. Something is wrong. Really wrong.

"How do I help?" Duncan asks.

"I don't know," I say, breathing through the pain. The hairs on the back of my neck rise onto the end and icicles trail along my skin. I look back the way we came, sensing an impending threat.

A thick white fog rolls across the flatland towards us. It's moving fast, too fast for a normal fog.

Terror makes the pain in my guts worse, but I manage to croak one word. "Run."

"You can't," he says.

I force myself up. I'm bawling; the pain is so bad it's almost blinding but I know that fog is bad. I can't let it catch me.

"We have to go." I grunt through the pain. "Now. Now."

I pull on his arm, stumbling forward. I can't run, but I can move. I concentrate to make one foot move then the other. He supports me but the pain keeps growing worse. I had food poisoning once and that is the closest thing I can compare this to.

"You cannae go on like this," Duncan says.

Despite the freezing rain, I'm burning up. I can't stand up straight, the cramps are so bad. I look over my shoulder and fear clamps onto my chest.

"We can't outrun it," I pant.

Ahead of us, echoes the sounds of battle, same as it did when I first arrived here. I don't know what the fog is going to do to me this time, but every time it comes, everything changes. I'm not ready for a change. Not now. I've chosen Duncan; I can't leave him.

"It's only a fog, coming down from the Highlands," Duncan says. "It's nothing."

"No. No, it's something more. Worse. I don't know what it is but, Duncan..." I grip his shoulders, leaning on him to keep myself upright. "No matter what happens, be safe. Live. Do you hear me? You live. Don't be a fool. Don't get yourself killed."

"Quinn, you talk as if you're leaving."

The fog rolls over us and our legs disappear in its thick white soup. It rolls in still faster. Desperate, I throw my arms around his neck and cling to him. He wraps his strong arms tight around me, but I know it won't be enough. I know it in my heart and it's killing me.

I sob in his ear. "I don't know what will happen, but you live, okay? For me?"

"Aye, Quinn," he says as the fog swamps us.

A force pulls me away from him, trying to rip me from his grip. We clench each other tighter, trying to hold on. One heartbeat. Two. My hands sweat profusely and my fingers slip. I inhale to call out to him, but his fingers slide free and I'm alone. Lost in the whiteness.

Chapter Thirty-Two

"DUNCAN!" I scream.

My throat is sore and raw. Every breath is painful. My voice is muffled by the fog, and no response comes. The cramping pain eases until at last it's gone.

I wander, directionless, calling for Duncan but getting no response. The white grows brighter when I take the next step. I emerge from the fog onto bright green grass, open blue skies, and a beautiful view on the top edge of a highland cliff.

"Duncan?" I ask, my voice more of a croak than my own.

I'm not where I left him. We were heading into the lowlands, towards Glen Fruin, but I'm back in the Highlands now. I shield my eyes with one hand and turn a slow circle, trying to find my bearings. Off to my left are white awnings.

"Oh no," I gasp.

Tents. White tents.

I'm back.

I don't try to hold back my tears as a fresh, raw pain explodes in my chest. It's not physical so much as emotional. I'm back in my time. Back where I started.

"Was it a dream?" I sob aloud, but when I take a step forward and the heavy skirts kick out in front of me, I know it wasn't.

I run my hands over the rough cloth of the skirt Alesoun gave me and cry harder. Did I do enough? Did I save him? Is he...?

No. I can't even think of it. He had to have lived. Had to. A black spiral of depression opens in my mind, so I move to avoid falling into it.

My friends and colleagues are probably at the tents. They must be worried. God knows what I'm going to have to deal with when I get to them. How long have I been gone? Are the police looking for me?

A shadow passes over the ground in front of me, and I look up. A huge black bird glides overhead. As it passes, it caws and I recognize the cry of the raven.

Great, the Fae must still be keeping an eye on me.

Which means it was real. The clothes I'm wearing should have been proof enough of that, but the raven is further confirmation. A wild storm of thoughts and emotions swirls in my head, fueling the black spiral that would be entirely too easy to give in to. The moment I do, I'll either be locked away or put on medication to numb it all away.

Exactly as the Fae were talking about. Our modern society is really all about quiet. No matter how much we rant and rave on social media, it's rare anyone *does* something and when they do, they're quickly silenced.

Our lives are spent on screens. Televisions, computers, and the ever-present cell phones. And when we get too far astray, there's plenty of chemical assistance to balance you out. To keep you calm. Keep you quiet. Keep you from dreaming too much or too loudly.

I had a friend who was an artist. She was a beautiful dreamer, but she was always stressed. Always worried about everything. And when she was put on medication, all her drive to create art was gone. She tried, but she said it didn't hold her interest anymore. She became an accountant.

As I confront my fears and emotions, I find something I didn't expect: resolve. I've been ripped from my world and thrust into another. A life that on its surface is much harder, but one where the people still dream. They hold true to ancient ways, and they believe. Believe in the Fae and in each other.

A life where I found a man I can love.

Duncan. I see him so clearly in my head. Even just from the memory of him, my body flushes. He could, with a single look, make me feel like the only girl in the world. It was special.

And having found him, having found the love of my life, I've been ripped back here. The Fae Queen named me Destroyer. Well, if that's what it takes, then I'm going to destroy whatever gets in my way. I don't know how, yet, but I know one thing: I'm getting back to him.

Hitching up my skirt, I stride forward to meet destiny head-on.

Chapter Thirty-Three

IT HAS TAKEN three days of interrogations by both friends and officials to alleviate everyone's concerns about my disappearance.

I excuse my absence by telling them I was lost in the fog. This of course led them to asking about my clothes. I've never been much of a liar, but I was creative enough when put on the spot. I told them I found a lady living alone who took care of me until I could find my way back. My story is lame. I know it, they know it, but since no one can prove anything different, they've had to accept it. Time travel. Huh. Who knew it would be so difficult? In this place and time, I was missing for three days. It doesn't matter that I spent weeks with the MacGregors. I guess the old stories are true; time runs differently when the Fae are involved.

An empty ache throbs in my guts as I watch the Highlands roll by outside the van window. The mood is subdued, much quieter than when we arrived. I don't want to leave, but I know I must.

"I can't believe you were lost for so long," Savannah says for probably the millionth time. "I would have been terrified. I was so scared that you were gone forever, like that missing person poster. Who was it?"

Savannah hasn't let me out of her sight since my return except for while I was being interrogated by the authorities. She won't even let me shower alone, sitting on the toilet while I do.

"Michael, that was his name," Gail throws in. "Michael MacGregor."

It takes a moment to register what they're talking about but then I remember the poster we saw at the train station when we arrived. A few days for them, but it's been weeks for me.

"Fortunately not," I say. I try to make my smile reassuring, but my thoughts are so far away from here, it's hard.

"There were search parties and everything," Savannah goes on.

"Yeah," I agree. "Sorry, I didn't mean to cause such a fuss."

I've said sorry a lot since my return. My classmates keep expressing their concerns, which I appreciate. The thing is, I don't feel sorry. I haven't really felt anything since my return. This world seems less real than it did. It's unimportant, like we're all living in a thinning façade and if I look too closely, I'll see the flaws and cracks in what we all accept as reality. As I did in the Fae realms. Like I'm walking in a perfect glamour, but don't look. When you look, everything falls apart.

Savannah places her arm over my shoulders and slides across the bench seat of the van, holding me tight. Professor Galmatin is sitting in the front behind the driver and even he is oddly quiet. He has barely spoken since my return. I can't imagine the stress he was under with losing a student under his care. I don't think he has recovered yet. Probably be the last trip abroad he takes.

I stare out the window as the van trundles down the road, taking us to the airport. I'm connected to this land. Its grip on my heart is no longer tenuous and definitely not imaginary. There is a phantom pain as if ice cold fingers grip my soul and it's being stretched as we race away.

Duncan. Live. You have to live.

Empty fields roll past, delineated by a long running fence with evenly spaced posts. A raven sits on top of a post. As we pass, I lock eyes with it. It caws and I hear it in my head more than with my ears.

The fae isn't done with me yet.

That's okay. I'm not done with them either.

"I'm really glad you're okay," Savannah says softly. "Seriously, I was so scared. How am I supposed to live without you?"

I force myself to tear my eyes off the passing countryside. We're leaving the highlands behind, the fields flattening and giving way to farmland which makes it somehow easier. This isn't the land that has a hold on my soul.

"Me too," I say, honestly.

"That fog was so thick," Savannah says. "I tried to find you then at last they made us take shelter before the storm broke. I can't believe you were out there alone. And you found a hermit lady. How strange is that?"

"I'm glad I did," I say. "I don't know how I would have survived without Alesoun."

"You're home now. That's what matters."

"Home," I say, a deep, melancholic sadness blanketing my heart.

I hold back the tears by swallowing hard and looking away. Did Duncan survive? Did any of them? How do I get back? I'm going to; there is no question of that. The only question is how?

I close my eyes and rest my head against the window. The vibrations from the humming tires are soothing as I let my thoughts drift.

I'm at a crossroads but this time neither path is clear. I have to choose, but in my heart, I know no matter which one I do, there are going to be consequences. What are they? How do I choose when I don't know?

"Are you okay?" Savannah asks, her voice far away.

"Yeah," I say, not opening my eyes and thereby not leaving the crossroads in my mind. "Just thinking."

"What about?"

"Choices. The choices we make and the consequences of them."

"Heavy thoughts."

"I know. How do you choose the path forward when you don't know the consequences?"

She grabs my hand, pulling me back into the now with her. She stares, her eyes glistening, and the depth of understanding and knowledge in them is surprising. The sun reflects through the window, outlining her with a golden halo and in the moment, Savannah seems to be part of my dreams of other times and realms of fae.

"You follow your heart. That's all you can do. It's all any of us can do."

"My heart?"

Her smile is dazzling, pulling the rays of light and reflecting them back like a prism, rainbows dancing off her lips and accenting her words.

"Your heart," she says, touching my cheek. Warmth spreads out from her touch.

"Savannah, are you...?"

I trail off as the sun shifts and the beatific glow is gone. Savannah is herself, my friend exactly as I've always known her.

"You okay?" she asks.

I nod. "I will be."

Chapter Thirty-Four

THE LIGHT of the laptop screen glares off the pure white page and black words, stabbing them into my brain like so many daggers. I close my eyes and rub them then massage my temples, trying to ease the throbbing pain.

"Damn it." I lean back in my office chair, tilting until I'm staring up at the ceiling. "Damn it!"

My dorm neighbor pounds on the wall and gives a muffled yell. "Sorry. Sorry."

I run my fingers through my hair, scratching at my scalp, then in a fit of pent-up energy burst out of the chair and pace the room. It's four paces long and two wide, not counting my desk, bed, and mini-fridge, so pacing is a loose term for what I'm doing.

I've been home a month, back in my dorm and nothing is the same. What happened to me feels less real with every passing day. What was vivid memory is taking on a dreamlike quality that makes me question if it's real or not. The only thing that is real is what I see every time I close my eyes. The memory of Duncan dying. Every time it plays, my heart is blasted apart. Every time, it tears its way through, opening the wounds anew.

We didn't stop it, damn it. The Fae were right. Nothing in the history books has changed. Or it wasn't real.

I stop mid-pace and give a hateful glare to the stack of books next to my laptop. The offending histories, all the websites, everything I've checked, agrees. History is what it was. The MacGregors name was outlawed. They were massacred in droves. Unspeakable atrocities were committed against them.

What none of them are telling me, not one book, not one website, not even genealogy.com, is the one thing I want to know: did he survive?

Was he real? Was any of them real?

I grab Mr. Buttons, my stuffed bear that my mom gave me when I was six, off my bed. I hold him up and examine his roughness. He has been patched so many times, I don't think there's an original stitch still in him. One button eye has been replaced and doesn't match the other in hue even if the overall color is correct. He's rough, like Duncan.

"It's not like it's not already bad enough," I mutter to Mr. Buttons. "Either I'm insane, or I'm in love with a man who was born four hundred years ago. Either one or the other is enough of a barrier to overcome, wouldn't you say?"

I drop onto the edge of my bed and clutch Mr. Buttons to my chest, just like I did when I was a kid. I hang my head and tears fall. The empty ache in my chest grows in intensity until I have to let it out somehow. Tears are better than any alternative because it really feels like if I let the pressure go, it will explode out of my chest like an alien spawn.

"What do I do?" I ask Mr. Buttons.

Grabbing my phone off my side table I stare at my contacts and debate calling home. A tingling sensation in my head makes that feel like a bad idea. I don't know why, but for whatever reason, I don't. I put the phone down and lie on my back.

The ceiling of my dorm room is a drop, with those rectangular foam looking squares covered in squiggly lines. I don't know if they're supposed to be a design or if its part of the manufacturing process that makes them. They're boring. Someone knocks at the door, and I push myself up onto my elbows. The knock repeats so I get up, run my fingers through my hair and rub my face, then open the door.

"Hey," Savannah says.

"Hi," I say.

"Coffee?"

"Isn't it late for that?" I ask.

"Decaf?" she grins.

"Why not?" I grab my wallet and a sweater off the back of my desk chair then join her.

We walk across the wide-open campus. I don't bother looking around. Before Scotland I thought the Missouri University campus was big and sprawling. Now I know it's flat, cramped, and doesn't have a single breathtaking view. We cross a street to a popular coffee shop, *Redux*. Even though its past eight at night the shop is busy. College students aren't known for keeping regular hours.

We get our drinks and slip into a corner booth. Some alt band plays over the hidden speakers creating just enough noise along with the buzz of conversation to create a feeling of privacy, real or imagined I don't know.

"How are you?" Savannah asks and I shrug, forcing a half smile. She reaches across the table and grasps my arm, squeezing until I meet her eyes. "Seriously."

"Fine," I say but it's a lie and we both know it.

I'm exhausted. Distracted. I haven't been the same since my adventure. I don't know why I'm back here. Why the Fae haven't contacted me. Or, really, what do with myself. Nothing feels quite real, as if I'm less alive than I was when I was with the MacGregors.

"It's been a month." Savannah takes a sip of her coffee then sighs and stares across the shop. We sit in silence that isn't exactly uncomfortable. When she looks back she shrugs. "I miss you."

"I'm right here."

"No," she says, sadness in her eyes and voice.

"What do you mean?"

"I don't know," she says. "You're different. Distracted, sure. Stressed, I guess. I can't imagine what you've gone through but..." she trails off, takes a deep breath then exhales is sharply. "I'm here, Quinn. If you need someone to talk to, I'm here."

I don't have to force my smile as I reach across the table and cover her hand with my own.

"Thank you."

She puts her other hand on top of mine.

"Your Mom was Scottish, right?"

"Yeah," I say. "She grew up in America, but her parents immigrated from Scotland."

The empty ache in my chest returns. My head is throbbing, and the coffee isn't helping. I rub my temples to try and ease the pressure.

"You remember that bird?"

"The raven? Yeah, why?"

It's an odd question and one I didn't expect. It's too close to what happened to me for comfort too which makes me nervous.

"I thought about it earlier today. I kept seeing a black bird around campus and I'd swear it was the same one. That's impossible of course. I looked it up on Wikipedia, ravens don't fly that far, but still it was pretty crazy."

My breath catches in my chest and I cough to cover my surprise. Savannah, though, doesn't miss my reaction. Her eyes narrow and she frowns.

"You don't think?"

"No, it's impossible," I say, sipping my coffee to give myself time to recover.

Rikki? Could it be? Is he looking for me? If he is, does that mean Dugald is close?

225

"You're right," she laughs. "It would be cool, though. Wouldn't it? Kind of romantic?"

"Romantic?"

"Yeah, you know, the raven is looking for someone. Maybe it's a handsome Highlanders pet and he'd show up all buff and shirtless, with long flowing brown hair and bulging muscles all over the place. Ready to sweep me, I mean someone off their feet."

"Me, huh? Sounds like you've got this figured out."

"Nah," she says. "Well, in fantasy I suppose. In reality, though? We're archaeologist, if that's taught me anything, life in olden times was anything but golden. It was hard work, no entertainment, and an early death for most."

"Right," I nod, but the cold in my guts is chilling because I know firsthand how right she is.

Life was hard back then. Death was imminent for everyone, a constant companion that you could meet turning a corner. Yet, they were alive. I was alive. Engaged, the world full of color and magic. Real magic.

Magic that, supposedly, I have will decide to save or not. When all I really care about is saving one clan, one man, but I have a 'destiny'. Or I'm crazy.

My trip through time has taken on an unreal, dreamlike aspect. I've had doubts if it was real or not. Maybe I hit my head. Maybe someone slipped something into my food or drink, and I had a delayed reaction to it.

We make small talk while finishing our coffee than walk back to the dorms. She's in a different hall than I am so we stand on the commons and visit a little longer while the sun finishes setting. Surreptitiously I keep checking the skies, hoping to see a large black bird, but to no avail. We share a last parting hug, then I return to my room. At least now I have at least a glimmer of hope.

A raven is looking and if I'm sure of anything, I'm sure of this. It's looking for me.

Chapter Thirty-Five

I'M OBSTINATELY TRYING to study for a test and it's almost midnight when a sound penetrates my concentration. Bleary eyed and exhausted I look away from the computer screen and around for the source. The sound pulls at my attention without being too intrusive.

Tap. Tap. Tap.

What the hell?

I stand up and turn a slow circle. My dorm room is too tiny to take more than an instant to survey it all. I move to the wall by my desk. The same wall that the neighboring student pounds on to shut up my random outbursts. I press my ear to the wall and listen.

Tap. Tap. Tap.

No, it's not the neighboring students. Frowning, I stand up straight and close my eyes to listen. It comes again so I move, one step at a time, until I close in with the sound.

The window.

I pull the thick curtain aside and soft silver moonlight streams in. A dark patch on the windowsill holds my attention. I unlock the window then fight to get it to open. It only comes up three or four inches. I hold it in place with my left hand and reach through with my right, grabbing the dark object. I pull it in and when I let the window go, it slams back into place barely missing my fingers.

I hold the object up, and the moonlight glistens along its delicate edge. A black feather. I hold it by the quill, turning it over and letting the light refract off. A raven caws in my mind. This is it. The sign I've been looking for.

All I experienced was real. Duncan, Alesoun, even hateful old Agnes MacGregor. It was real and I'm being called back.

I'm going to get back there.

I lean over the bed and look out the window. The black shape of a bird crosses over the moon and my heart soars with it. When I look down at the yard, I see a dark figure staring up at my window. My heart leaps into a gallop. I gasp and jerk back, dropping the curtain.

"No way," I mutter.

Shifting around until I'm squeezed between the bed and the wall, I peek out the window again. The figure is still down there, and its head shifts towards the side I'm peeking out.

"Son of a—"

I slide on my slippers and run out of my dorm room. I take the stairs down two at a time. When I reach the second landing, my foot slips and I slam into the wall. I get an arm up in time to protect my head but there's going to be fresh bruises tomorrow.

The security guard at his desk barely looks up from his phone as I pass. I slam into the door at a dead run but don't hit the release bar firmly and bounce off it with a yelp.

"You have to—"

"I know," I shout, cutting him off and slowing down enough to open the door successfully.

The 'yard' is a large concrete patio surrounded by strategically placed benches on its edges. A sculpture sits in the middle of the space, modernistic and interpretive in design. I've always looked at it as a wave caught in mid-motion. The half-moon illuminates the sculpture and casts shadows across the open court that flutter as clouds pass over the moon.

Dugald stands perfectly tucked into one of those shadows. I stop directly in front of him.

"Did he live?" I ask, heart pounding, blood rushing in my ears.

Dugald's face is hidden in shadow. He doesn't speak but I feel his stare and see the glint of his eyes in the shadows.

"Well? Answer me."

"Hello, Quinn."

"Did. He. Live?" I bite off each word, ignoring his attempt at pleasantries.

He doesn't respond. He doesn't even blink.

Angry energy thrums, making me feel as if I'm vibrating. I have to know. "Well?"

He looks away then steps backwards into the deeper shadows.

"Be careful what you wish for, Quinn."

"What does that mean? Answer the question."

He shakes his head. "I cannot."

"Cannot or will not?"

He shakes his head. "I wanted to see if you are okay."

"If I'm okay?" I ball my hands into fists, shaking. "Do I look okay? I can't focus. I can't quit thinking about it. None of it mattered if I didn't change anything!"

"You're wrong," he whispers. "You changed everything."

"I have to go back."

"I'll see you soon, Destroyer."

He steps back again and he's gone, swallowed by the shadows.

"Dugald?" I ask, stepping into the shadow after him but they're empty. Nothing.

I walk around the statue looking for him, but he's gone like a puff of smoke in a breeze. Giving up finding him, I look up at the silvery moon which resembles a half-closed eye lazily gazing with no real interest.

A chilly breeze whistles around the concrete statue causing me to shiver. I rub my arms and close my eyes.

It was real. I'm not crazy.

"I will find a way back. I will find Duncan. If I can go back in time once, I can do it again."

A vaguely defined thrumming echoes through my core. It reminds me of the power I gathered in the fae lands, power I haven't felt since. As the thrumming grows stronger, the shadows cast by the moonlight sharpen, taking on more defined lines and shapes, and I feel it. That same malevolent awareness in the darkness. An intention that can only come with consciousness.

My nails dig into my palms and the pain sharpens my focus. I turn my back on the pensive shadows and stride back into my dormitory. Before I walk back into the building, I stop and turn to confront the darkness.

"I'm coming, Duncan. No matter what it takes. I'll get back to you. I swear it."

* * *

Ready for the next part of the story?
Book 2 - Exiled from the Highlands

* * *

If you'd like to read something else by Miranda, check out Dragon's Baby (Red Planet Dragons of Tajss Book 1), a sci-fi alien dragon warrior romance.

Join Miranda's Reader List

USA TODAY BESTSELLING AUTHOR

Subscribe to get the Red Planet Dragons of Tajss prequel Dragon's Origins *PLUS* bonus freebie Ribbed For Her Pleasure!

http://www.mirandamartinromance.com/newsletter

DO YOU WANT NSFW ART, FREE BOOKS, AND BE FIRST TO READ NEW CHAPTERS?

http://www.patreon.com/immirandamartin

About Miranda Martin

USA Today bestselling author Miranda Martin writes fantasy and scifi romance featuring heroes with out-of-this-world anatomy that readers call 'larger than life' and smart heroines destined to save the world. As a little girl, she would sneak off with her nose in a book, dreaming of magical realms. Today she brings those fantasies to life and adores every fan who chooses to live in them for a while.

Though born and raised in southern Virginia, Miranda Martin is a veteran who's traveled to places like Korea, Hawaii, and good 'ole Texas. She's since settled in Kansas, the heart of America, with her husband and daughters, a cat, and wishes for a pet dragon or unicorn. When she's not writing, you can still find her tucked away somewhere with a warm blanket and her nose in a book.

Visit her website http://mirandamartinromance.com

Made in the USA
Monee, IL
18 September 2022

14166629R00143